Study Guide to Accompany

Alan J. Auerbach and Laurence J. Kotlikoff

MACROECONOMICS
An Integrated Approach

second edition

Study Guide to Accompany

Alan J. Auerbach and Laurence J. Kotlikoff

MACROECONOMICS
An Integrated Approach

second edition

prepared by
Debra Moore Patterson

The MIT Press
Cambridge, Massachusetts
London, England

Contents

Prologue: The Question of Macroeconomics

Prologue Outline

Introduction

An integrated approach to macroeconomics

Modeling macroeconomic behavior

The life-cycle model

Evaluating economic theories

Summary

Key Terms

Economic model
Life-cycle model
Macroeconomics
Natural experiment

PART ONE: FROM MICRO TO MACRO: MODELING INCOME DETERMINATION AND GROWTH

Chapter 1: Output, Inputs, and Growth

Chapter Outline

Introduction

How economic growth affects living standards

Modeling production
        The Cobb-Douglas production function
        Getting acquainted with the Cobb-Douglas production function

Measuring capital
        An aside: The relationship of stocks to flows

Measuring labor

The role of multifactor productivity
        Case study: How does productivity grow?

Accounting for growth
        Case study: Sources of U.S. growth since 1948

Labor productivity
        Does labor productivity influence workers' pay?

What explains the U.S. labor productivity slowdown?
        The role of capital deepening
        Other causes of the productivity slowdown
                A changing production mix
                Changes in the quality of capital and labor
                Declining research and development
                Government regulation
        Summary: Why has growth in U.S. labor productivity slowed?

Is the United States becoming the poor kid on the block?

Is the gap between rich and poor countries widening?

Chapter summary

Key Terms

Capital
Cobb-Douglas production function
Depreciation
Flow variable
Gross domestic product (GDP)
Growth accounting
Investment
Labor
Labor force
Labor productivity
Multifactor productivity
Production function
Standard of living
Stock variable
Technology

Key Equations

General production function: $Y_t = f(A_t, K_t, L_t)$

Cobb-Douglas production function: $Y_t = A_t K_t^\beta L_t^{(1-\beta)}$, where $0 < \beta < 1$

Growth rate of output (approximation): $\Delta Y/Y = \Delta A/A + \beta \Delta K/K + (1-\beta) \Delta L/L$

Labor productivity: $y = A k^\beta$

4

QUESTIONS FOR CHAPTER 1

Review Questions

1. What is *real* GDP? How is real GDP calculated? What term is used to describe an increase in real GDP? a decrease?

2. What is the difference between a *stock* and a *flow*? How are the two related? Classify the following as either a stock or a flow: the size of the labor force; investment; depreciation; real GDP; an office building; the current state of technology.

3. What is a *production function*? How is the *Cobb-Douglas* production function written? To what does each of the variables refer? Provide an economic interpretation of the exponents.

4. What do economists mean when they refer to *labor* and *capital*? How is each typically measured?

5. Define *gross investment, net investment,* and *depreciation*. How are the three concepts related? How do the three help determine the size of the capital stock?

6. What is *multifactor productivity* and how is it measured in the Cobb-Douglas production function? What is the difference between *embodied* and *disembodied* productivity change? Give some examples of each.

7. To what extent have changes in the amounts of labor and capital and in multifactor productivity contributed to U.S. real GDP growth in the business sector during the past 50 years?

8. Define *labor productivity*. How does labor productivity differ from the *marginal product of labor*? How is the marginal product of labor affected by an increase in the amount of labor? in the amount of capital?

9. What is the recent record of labor productivity growth in the United States? What are some potential explanations of the recent trend?

10. How do economists measure the *standard of living*? How has the U.S. standard of living changed over the past few decades? How has this performance compared to the changes observed in other countries?

Numerical Questions

1. Suppose that U.S. real GDP is expected to grow by 2.5 percent per year.
    a.   If real GDP is currently $7 trillion, what will real GDP equal in ten years?
    b.   2.5 percent of $7 trillion is $0.175 trillion. If real GDP grows by $0.175 trillion per year, it will equal $8.75 trillion after ten years. Is your answer to part a greater than or less than $8.75 trillion? Why?

2. Suppose that a company currently owns two types of capital: two copy machines and eight personal computers. All the capital is new. Expressed in 1992 dollars, copiers cost $1,000 each and personal computers cost $800 each.
    a.   What is the total amount of capital owned by the company?
    b.   Suppose that copy machines depreciate at the rate of 20 percent per year and computers at the rate of 40 percent per year. (Helpful hint: The annual amount of depreciation D_t, for a particular type of capital equals the capital's depreciation rate in decimal form times the existing amount of that capital, K_t.) What will the company's capital stock be in two years?
    c.   Assume the same initial values of capital calculated in part a and the same depreciation rates as in part b. If the company buys another computer at the end of year 1, what will its total capital stock be at the end of year 2?

3. Output of the Chip Off the Old Block granite company is given by a Cobb-Douglas production function in which, for 1998, capital is 400, labor is 100, multifactor productivity is 5, and the exponents on capital and labor are 0.3 and 0.7, respectively.
    a.   What is the initial level of output?
    b.   What is the total compensation paid to the employees of the firm?
    c.   Does Chip Off the Old Block's production function exhibit constant returns to scale? (Helpful hint: Increase both capital and labor by 50 percent and observe the resulting change in output.)
    d.   Suppose that between 1998 and 1999 output grows by 2.5 percent, capital grows by 1 percent, and labor grows by 2 percent. What must have been the growth rate of multifactor productivity over the year?

4. Annual output of the Every Day Is Sundae ice cream company is given by a Cobb-Douglas production function in which capital is 200, labor is 100, multifactor productivity is 2, and the exponents on capital and labor are 0.4 and 0.6, respectively.

    a.   Calculate the ice cream company's labor productivity using the *intensive* form of the production function.

    b.   Suppose that Every Day Is Sundae doubles its ratio of capital to labor. Compute the impact on labor productivity.

    c.   Does your answer to part b depend on *how* the ratio is doubled? That is, does it matter whether the capital stock doubles or the labor force is cut in half?

    d.   Suppose the company's multifactor productivity rises to 3 from 2, while capital and labor remain at their initial values of 200 and 100, respectively. Calculate the impact of the multifactor productivity change on labor productivity.

5.   Suppose that an economy's production is described by a Cobb-Douglas production function in which the exponents on capital and labor are 0.3 and 0.7, respectively. Answer the questions in parts a and b, given the following data.

Year	Multifactor Productivity	Capital	Labor
1988	10	1000	500
1998	11	1100	600

    a.   Calculate output in each year and its percentage change during 1998.

    b.   What proportion of total output growth is accounted for by growth in multifactor productivity? by growth in capital? by growth in labor? (Recall that the formula for growth accounting is an approximation, so the percent change in output may slightly exceed the sum of the contributions of the three components.)

Analytical Questions

1.   Using the growth accounting framework, explain how the following economic policies would affect the economy's ability to produce output and why.

    a.   Congress votes to increase spending on public infrastructure.

    b.   Congress passes a law that limits the amount of immigration.

    c.   The president succeeds in convincing Congress to pass an investment tax credit that reduces the price of plant and equipment by 10 percent.

    d.   Congress relaxes antitrust laws to permit greater cooperation between firms in research and development endeavors.

e.   The Occupational Safety and Health Administration imposes new restrictions on the layout of factory floors.

2.   The text identified certain developing countries whose living standards were approaching those of developed countries, and others whose living standards were not. Some analysts have argued that countries that have not seen their living standards converge have suffered because their economies are based on centralized decision making and state ownership rather than free markets and private ownership. Evaluate this idea within the context of the growth accounting model. (Helpful hint: How might greater reliance on free markets and private ownership affect the factors underlying growth?)

3.   The following is a tabular representation of a Cobb-Douglas production function. The numbers along the top indicate varying amounts of labor; the numbers down the side indicate varying amounts of capital. The number in each cell in the table gives the amount of output produced for given amounts of capital and labor. For instance, if labor is 400 and capital is 10, then 264.53 units of output are produced. Answer the questions in parts a through c using the data in the table.

Capital	Labor		
	400	800	1200
10	264.53	429.73	570.76
20	325.67	529.06	702.69
30	367.80	597.49	793.58

a.   Using the data, give examples of diminishing returns to labor and of diminishing returns to capital.

b.   Suppose the development of a revolutionary and powerful computer chip raises multifactor productivity by 5 percent. How would such a development affect the data in the table?

c.   Does the production function represented in the table exhibit constant returns to scale? Answer by referring to specific numbers.

Chapter 2: The Dynamic Supply of Inputs

Chapter Outline

Introduction

Who owns and supplies inputs?
> *Case study:* Who "owns" the U.S. private capital stock?

The two-period life-cycle model
> The model's basic structure

Dynamic input supplies

The lifetime budget constraint

Present values
> *Case study:* You can't "win" if you don't play.

The saving decision
> A closer look at the consumption and saving decision
> A graphical depiction of Franco's consumption and saving decision

National saving equals national investment
> *Case study:* The decline in U.S. saving and its impact on domestic investment

Expanding the model to include variations in labor supply
> *Case study:* The worldwide demographic transition and the relative supplies of
> capital and labor

Chapter summary

Key Terms

> Compound interest
> Financial assets
> Human capital
> Indifference curve
> Liability

Life-cycle model
Lifetime budget constraint
Marginal rate of substitution (MRS)
National investment
National saving
Net foreign investment
Physical capital
Present-value discounting
Real assets
Utility function

Key Equations

Lifetime budget constraint: $\qquad c_{yt} + c_{ot+1}/(1+r_{t+1}) = w_t$

Cobb-Douglas utility function: $\qquad u_t = c_{yt}^{\alpha} c_{ot+1}^{1-\alpha} \qquad 0 < \alpha < 1$

National saving: $\qquad S_t = Y_t - N\,c_{yt} - N\,c_{ot}$

National investment: $\qquad I_t = K_{t+1} - K_t$

Key Graphs

Lifetime budget constraint:

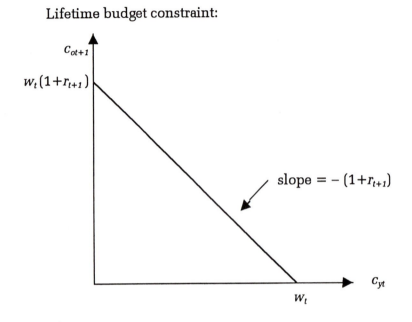

Utility maximizing consumption choice:

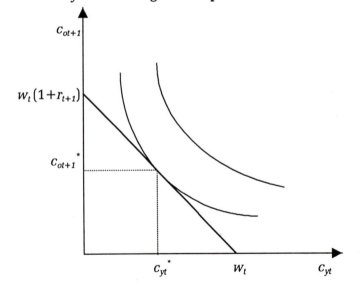

QUESTIONS FOR CHAPTER 2

Review Questions

1. What is *human capital*? Who owns human capital? What factors determine the amount of available human capital?

2. Who owns *physical capital*? What is the difference between direct ownership and indirect ownership of physical capital? Give an example of each.

3. What is the difference between *real assets* and *financial assets*? How can the income generated by a real asset represent both a financial *asset* and a financial *liability*? How is a country's *domestic net worth* calculated?

4. Give two definitions of the term "saving."

5. In the two-period life-cycle model, what activities do *young people* undertake? What activities do *old people* undertake?

6. Write the life-cycle model variables representing consumption, the wage, the interest rate (return on capital), and the number of young people and of old people. Use those variables to define a young person's saving; an old person's assets; the total labor force; the total capital stock; an old person's consumption. Be careful to use appropriate and consistent time subscripts in each case.

7. In what sense is a young person's decision about how much to spend when young also a decision about how much to save when young and how much to consume when old?

8. Use the symbols of the model to write an individual's *lifetime budget constraint*. Which variables in the constraint are outside an individual's control? Over which variables can an individual exercise choice? Describe in words the information provided by the lifetime budget constraint. What does a graph of the budget constraint look like?

9. What is the *present value* of a future payment? To what does the term *discounting* refer?

10. What information does a *utility function* provide? How is the *Cobb-Douglas* utility function written for present and future consumption? What aspect of the Cobb-Douglas utility function describes a person's *time preference*?

11. What are *indifference curves*? What is the *marginal rate of substitution*?

12. Explain why, in the life-cycle model, total saving in the economy equals total investment.

13. What is *net foreign investment*? How has U.S. net foreign investment behaved over the past several decades?

14. What changes in the age distribution of the U.S. population can be expected over the next 40 years? What implications might these have for future capital-labor ratios?

Numerical Questions

1. Suppose that you can reasonably expect a return of 5 percent on any investment that you make.
   a. If someone gives you $100 today, what will that $100 be worth in six years?
   b. If someone promises to pay you $100 three years from now, what is that promised payment worth to you today?
   c. Suppose that you are promised three payments: $10 in one year; $40 in two years; and $20 in three years. What is the *year 2* value of the promised payments?
   d. What is the present value of $200 paid three years from now if the interest rates over the three years are 5 percent, 7 percent, and 9 percent, respectively?

Use the following information to answer questions 2 through 5: $A = 4$, $K_0 = 300$, $N = 200$, $\alpha = 0.5$, and $\beta = 0.3$.

2. a. What is the value of output in period 0?
   b. How much income is paid to labor (i.e., to all workers combined)?
   c. How much income is received by an individual worker?
   d. What is the total income earned by capital?
   e. What is the interest rate? (Helpful hint: Remember that the total income earned by capital equals $r_t K_t$.)
   f. What are the values of consumption and saving by the young generation, given the amount of income computed in the previous question?

3.   Answer the following questions about economic activity in period 1.
      a.   What is the value of the *aggregate* capital stock in period 1?
      b.   Compute *aggregate* investment in period 1.
      c.   What is the value of production in period 1?
      d.   What is the value of each individual's lifetime income for those who are young in period 1?
      e.   What is the value of the interest rate in period 1?

4.   Answer the following questions regarding consumer utility.
      a.   What is the value of consumption by the old in period 1?
      b.   What is the value of utility of the generation born in period 0?

5.   Answer the following questions regarding the lifetime budget constraint.
      a.   Give the formula for the lifetime budget constraint.
      b.   What are the values of the vertical and horizontal intercepts of the budget constraint? Interpret these values.
      c.   What is the value of the slope? Interpret this value.
      d.   Verify that the combination of period 0 and period 1 consumption calculated above satisfies the lifetime budget constraint.

Analytical Questions

1.   What would be the effect on capital accumulation of a rise in the interest rate (r) offset by a reduction in lifetime income (w) that leaves an individual at the same level of utility?

2.   Disenchantment with the spending binge of the 1980s, sometimes called "the Decade of Greed," has led people to place greater weight on future consumption and well-being. How would such a development be reflected in the life-cycle model? What implications does this development have for the current level of investment and future levels of the capital stock and output?

3.   "The dynamic supply of capital depends on the dynamic evolution of the wage rate." Without using numbers, explain this statement.

4.   Consider a feasible consumption combination yielding a marginal rate of substitution of –1.05. If the rate of interest is 10 percent, should the individual raise or lower current consumption to achieve the optimal consumption combination?

5.   How would an advance in robotics be reflected in the life-cycle model? Without using numbers, describe the effect such a change might have on current period output, on total labor and capital income, and on the wage rate and interest rate.

Chapter 3: The Dynamic Demand for Inputs and the Evolution of Output

Chapter Outline

Introduction

Adding firms to our model

The capital structure of firms

The human capital structure of firms

Profit maximization
    The demand for capital and labor
    Cobb-Douglas input demands
    The relationship of the capital-labor ratio to the wage and the interest rate

The equilibrium values of the wage and the interest rate
    Diagramming factor market equilibrium

Modeling growth
    Using the transition equation to track the economy's growth path

Tracking the economy's growth path: a numerical example
    Where does the economy go and when does it get there?

Growth in the short and long runs
    The steady state
    Steady-state saving and investment

How growth affects the welfare of different generations
    Case study: Post-World War II Japanese and German capital deepening
    Case study: The black plague
    The transition path diagram
    Using the transition curve to track the time path of the capital-labor ratio
    Using the transition diagram to study changes in saving preferences

Adding population and technological change to our model
    Technological change: the study of endogenous growth

Chapter summary

Appendix 3A.1: Refresher on Exponents

Table 3A.1: Complete model for any time t

Key Terms

> Capital structure
> Dividends
> Endogenous growth
> Equity
> General equilibrium
> Marginal cost of capital
> Marginal cost of labor
> Marginal product of capital
> Marginal product of labor
> Pure profit
> Steady state
> Transition equation

Key Equations

> Aggregate profit: $\quad$ Profit $= Y - r\,K - w\,L$
>
> Equilibrium interest rate: $\quad r_{t+1} = \beta\,A_t\,k_t^{\beta-1}$
>
> Equilibrium wage: $\quad w_t = (1 - \beta)\,A_t\,k_t^{\beta}$
>
> Transition equation: $\quad k_{t+1} = (1 - \alpha)\,(1 - \beta)\,A_t\,k_t^{\beta}$

Table 3A.1 Complete Model for Any Time t

Labor supply equals the number of young	$L_t = N$
Capital supply equals the assets of the elderly	$K_t = Na_t$
Assets of the elderly equal their savings when young	$a_{t+1} = (1-\alpha)w_t$
Capital per worker is denoted by k	$k_t = K_t / L_t$
Output	$Y_t = A_t K_t^\beta L_t^{(1-\beta)}$
Marginal product of labor equals the wage	$w_t = (1-\beta)A_t k_t^\beta$
Marginal product of capital equals the interest rate	$r_t = \beta A_t k_t^{(\beta-1)}$
Transition equation	$k_{t+1} = (1-\alpha)(1-\beta)A_t k_t^\beta$
The young consume α of their wages	$c_{yt} = \alpha w_t$
The old consume their assets plus interest	$c_{ot} = a_t(1+r_t)$
National saving equals output less aggregate consumption	$S_t = Y_t - Nc_{yt} - Nc_{ot}$
National investment equals the increase in the capital stock	$I_t = K_{t+1} - K_t$

18

Key Graphs

Transition equation and steady state:

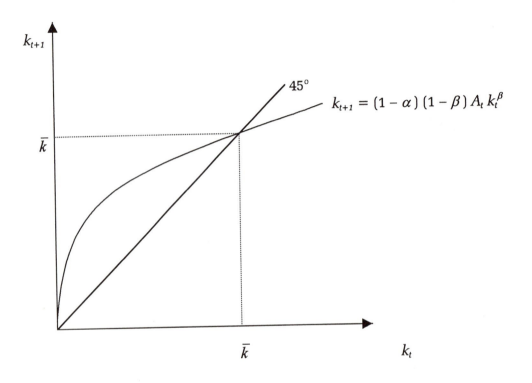

QUESTIONS FOR CHAPTER 3

Review Questions

1.   What are *equity* and *dividends*? Using notation from the life-cycle model, show how these factors relate to saving by the young and consumption by the elderly.

2.   If the elderly lend their savings to firms instead of purchasing ownership in firms, how does that affect the amount of consumption they can enjoy when they are old?

3. What is *capital structure*? Taking into account institutional factors such as bankruptcy laws, why might there be some differences between using debt finance and using equity finance?

4. How do the human capital assumptions used in the life-cycle model differ from human capital development in the real world?

5. To economists, what does the term *pure profit* mean? How does it differ from the term *profit* in everyday parlance? If pure profit is zero, are firms earning any return on their capital?

6. What is meant by *competitive input markets*? Specifically, what conditions lead input markets to be competitive, and what are the implications for factor prices?

7. What is the *marginal product of an input*? What is *marginal cost of an input*? Why must they be equal if profit is being maximized?

8. What happens to the value of the marginal product of capital as more capital is employed? Illustrate your answer using the intensive-form formulas for the marginal product. What is the term given to describe this property? Show whether the same property holds for increasing labor. Also show what impact an increase in capital has on the marginal product of *labor*.

9. What information is provided by the *transition equation*? Explain what is meant by the *steady state*. How can the transition equation help us determine how the economy looks in the steady state?

10. Why does growth ultimately cease when the labor force and technology are constant?

11. How does the life-cycle model help explain changes in the standard of living over time and other phenomena such as adjustments following loss of capital or labor due to extraordinary events such as war and plagues?

12. What distinguishes *endogenous growth* models from variants of the life-cycle model considered thus far?

20

Numerical Questions

Assume the following values when answering questions 1 through 6: $A = 4$, $N = 200$, $K_0 = 300$, $\alpha = 0.5$, and $\beta = 0.3$.

1.   a.   Calculate the equilibrium values of w_0 and r_0.
       b.   What happens to w_0 and r_0 if K_0 rises to 400?
       c.   What happens to w_0 and r_0 if N rises to 250?
       d.   What happens to w_0 and r_0 if β falls to 0.25?

2.   a.   Calculate the time path of k_t, K_t, Y_t, w_t, and r_t for periods 1 through 4.
       b.   What are the steady-state values of these variables?
       c.   What percent of the capital stock's transition to the steady state occurs between period 0 and period 1? between period 3 and period 4? Explain any difference.
       d.   At what rate will k_t, K_t, Y_t, w_t, and r_t grow in the steady state? Why?

2.   Suppose that the economy is currently in the steady state calculated in question 2. Congress suddenly alters immigration laws, causing an increase in N of 50.
       a.   Calculate the time path of k_t, K_t, Y_t, w_t, and r_t for the four periods after the change in N.
       b.   What are the new steady-state values of k_t, K_t, Y_t, w_t, and r_t?
       c.   Compare the new steady-state values to those before the change in N. Explain any differences and similarities.

4.   Once again, assume that the economy is currently in the steady state calculated in question 2. Suddenly a series of earthquakes destroys one-third of the capital stock.
       a.   Calculate the time path of k_t, K_t, Y_t, w_t, and r_t for the four periods after the change in the capital stock.
       b.   Calculate the new steady-state values of k_t, K_t, Y_t, w_t, and r_t.
       c.   Compare the new steady-state values of those before the change in the capital stock. Explain any differences and similarities.

5.   Using the initial values, graph the transition path. When drawing the graph, plot five points: two with k_t below its steady-state value, one with k_t equal to its steady state, and two with k_t above its steady-state value.
       a.   Explain why a 45-degree line can be used to locate the steady-state value of k_t.
       b.   How is an increase in α shown in the graph?

    c.   How is a decrease in A shown in the graph?
    d.   How is an increase in N shown in the graph?

6.   Suppose that β falls to 0.25.
    a.   Compute the new steady-state values for k_t, K_t, Y_t, w_t, and r_t.
    b.   Compare the new steady-state values to those computed in question 2. Explain any differences and similarities.

Analytical Questions

1.   Assuming that firms maximize profits and that the price of output is 1, why must the interest rate equal the marginal product of capital? Why must the wage rate equal the marginal product of labor?

2.   Using the formulas from the Cobb-Douglas production function (i.e., using variables rather than numbers), show that if factor prices equal their marginal products, then pure profit must be zero.

3.   In the life-cycle model, an increase in multifactor productivity has no effect on the steady-state value of r_t. Explain why this is so. (Helpful hint: A change in A_t has two effects on the marginal product of capital.)

4.   "A country's standard of living can continue to rise only if there is ongoing technological change." Comment.

5.   Many commentators have claimed that the high-spending, low-saving lifestyle of the 1980s will result in lower living standards for future generations. Use the life-cycle model to evaluate this claim.

Chapter 4: Economic Fluctuations

Chapter Outline

Introduction

What are economic fluctuations?
        The frequency, duration, and volatility of business cycles
        Case study: Has U.S. business cycle volatility really declined?

The anatomy of business cycles
        Sectoral versus general effects
        The cyclical volatility of major industries
        Case study: California's endless recession
        Timing of turning points: the index of leading indicators

Unemployment
        The household survey
        Employment and hours
        Capital becomes unemployed, too

Understanding economic fluctuations
        Uses of output over the cycle
        International spillovers
        The business cycle and the seasonal cycle
        Are business cycles actually cycles?

How do economic fluctuations fit into our model?
        The response of consumption and investment to a technology shock
        Does the real business cycle model explain economic fluctuations?

Chapter Summary

Key Terms

        Accelerator
        Business cycles
        Capacity utilization
        Consumption smoothing

Discouraged workers
Employed
Expansion
Labor force
Labor force participation rate
Leading indicator
Procyclical behavior
Random walk theory
Real business cycle theory
Recession
Seasonal adjustment
Turning point
Unemployment

Key Equations

Investment per worker: $i_t = (1 - \alpha)(1 - \beta)(y_t - y_{t-1})$

QUESTIONS FOR CHAPTER 4

Review Questions

1. Define the terms *expansion* and *recession*. How is the existence of a recession determined?

2. What are the relative lengths of expansions versus recessions? How have the average lengths of each changed over time?

3. How is business cycle *volatility* measured? Has volatility changed over time?

4. Why do macroeconomists try to distinguish broad-based, short-term cyclical fluctuations from long-term sectoral declines?

5. To what does the term *leading indicators* refer? What is the *Composite Index of Leading Indicators*? What shortcomings does the index have as a forecasting tool?

6. Define the terms *employed, unemployed, labor force, discouraged workers,* and *labor force participation rate.*

7. Identify three ways in which the economy's measured labor input declines during a recession.

8. How is the *utilization of capital* over the business cycle measured?

9. Are the timing and magnitude of business cycles similar across major industrialized countries?

10. What is *seasonal data adjustment*, and why do macroeconomists prefer to study seasonally adjusted data?

11. How does the *real business cycle theory* explain economic fluctuations?

12. What is the *accelerator*, and how does it arise in the life-cycle model?

13. What is *consumption smoothing*, and how does it arise in the life-cycle model?

Numerical Questions

1. Suppose that you are given the following information about the labor market. The amounts shown are in thousands.

Year	Population	Employment	Unemployment
1997	188,049	117,914	6874
1998	189,765	116,877	8426
1999	191,576	117,598	9384

   a. For each year, calculate the size of the labor force.
   b. For each year, calculate the labor force participation rate.
   c. For each year, calculate the unemployment rate.
   d. Do the data suggest that the number of discouraged workers might have increased in a particular year? If so, which year?

2. Assume that the economy starts out in a steady state characterized by the following values: $A = 4$, $N = 200$, $\alpha = 0.5$; and $\beta = 0.3$. Suppose that A rises *for only one period* to 4.5, and then returns to its initial value of 4.
   a. Trace out the resulting time path for the capital-labor ratio and total output over the next four periods.

b.   What are the new steady-state values for the capital-labor ratio and total output?

c.   In what sense does the path of output constitute a "business cycle"? In what sense does the output path not constitute a "business cycle"?

3.   Assume that output follows the same path as calculated in question 2.

     a.   For each of the four periods, compute investment per worker, i_t, and the percentage change from the preceding period.

     b.   For each of the four periods, compute c_t, total consumption divided by the number of young persons, and the percentage change from the preceding period.

     c.   Compare your answers in parts a and b to the percentage change in output per worker. Does investment per worker change by a greater or lesser amount than output per worker? What about consumption per person? Are your answers consistent with the concepts of the accelerator mechanism and consumption smoothing?

Analytical Questions

1.   Suppose that recent unemployment reports from the U.S. Department of Labor indicate that the unemployment rate has held steady at 7 percent for several months. Is it possible to draw firm conclusions about the health of labor markets from these reports? That is, is it possible that labor market conditions are actually improving despite the lack of change in the unemployment rate? Why or why not?

2.   You are a member of the President's Council of Economic Advisers and a strong believer in real business cycle theory. For the past several months, economic and financial data have indicated that real GDP is falling. The President has asked for your opinion about the correct policy response. What do you tell him?

3.   Assume that a country's economy is in a steady state. The country enters a war in period 1 which requires a fraction of the labor force to leave the country for one period. After that, the labor force returns to its original level. Answer the following without using numbers; it may help to refer to the transition diagram (Figure 3.8 in the text).

     a.   What happens in period 1 to the capital-labor ratio? to the level of output? to saving by the young and therefore next period's capital stock?

b.   In period 2, given the new value of the capital stock and the return of the labor force to the initial level, what happens to the capital-labor ratio? to the level of output relative to its steady-state value?

c.   Subsequent to period 2, what will the path of the capital-labor ratio look like?

d.   What will the path of output between the old steady state and the new steady state look like?

Chapter 5: The Measurement of Output and Prices

Chapter Outline

Introduction

Measuring gross domestic product
      Case study: How not to impose a sales tax

Related measures of production and Income
      GNP versus GDP
      Net domestic product and national income
      National income versus personal income

Components of GDP
      Consumption versus investment
      The treatment of housing
      Consumption of the services of government capital

Using the national income identity
      National saving and the trade deficit
      Case study: The trade deficit since 1980

Distinguishing real from nominal magnitudes
      Measuring inflation
      Using the CPI
      Biases in the CPI
            Commodity substitution
            New goods and quality change
      Reform of the CPI
      Measuring real GDP
      Case study: Biases in the measurement of real GDP
      An alternative measure of inflation

Adding nominal quantities to our model
      Measuring the real interest rate

Additional problems in measuring GDP
      Non-market activities
      Unreported income

28

Distorted markets
Pollution and other environmental damage

Chapter summary

Key Terms

Base year
Chain weighting
Circular flow diagram
Consumer price index (CPI)
Crowding out
Disposable income
Fisher equation
GDP deflator
Gross Domestic Product (GDP)
Gross National Product (GNP)
Imputed rent
Indexed bonds
Inflation rate
Market basket
National income
National income identity
Net foreign investment
Nominal interest rate
Personal income
Price index
Price level
Quantity index
Real interest rate
Trade balance
Trade deficit
Value added

Key Equations

Gross domestic product: $$GDP = C + I + G + X - M$$

Net foreign investment: $$I^f = X - M + Y^f$$

CPI:
$$CPI_{1997} = \frac{\sum\limits_{i=1}^{M} p^i_{1997} \times q^i_{1982-84}}{\sum\limits_{i=1}^{M} p^i_{1982-84} \times q^i_{1982-84}}$$

Fisher equation:
$$i_{t+1} = r_{t+1} + \pi_{t+1}$$

QUESTIONS FOR CHAPTER 5

Review Questions

1. How does the *circular flow of income* diagram help to explain the *national income identity*? Explain how the *final sales method* and the *factor incomes method* of computing GDP relate to your answer.

2. What is the difference between *final* and *intermediate* goods? Why aren't all sales by businesses included in GDP? What is the *value added method* for computing GDP?

3. What is the difference between *GDP* and *GNP*? Which one more closely reflects domestic business cycle behavior (i.e., within U.S. borders)? How large is the numerical difference between the two measures?

4. Explain how *gross domestic product, net domestic product, national income, personal income,* and *disposable income* are related.

5. How are corporate profits, retained earnings, and dividends related? Which are included in personal income?

6. What are the (expenditure) components of GDP? Why are imports subtracted from expenditures in summing to GDP? How are expenditures by individuals further broken down? What are some of the current inconsistencies in categorizing actual expenditures?

7. What is meant by *imputed rent*? How is it treated in the national income accounts?

8. Explain what is meant by a *quantity index* and why *real GDP* is an example of one. How does real GDP differ from *nominal GDP?*

9. Why is real GDP calculated using a *chain-weighted index?*

10. Explain what is meant by a *price index*. What is the difference between a *Laspeyres index* and a *Paasche index?* Give an example of each.

11. What is the *GDP deflator* and in what ways does it differ from the *Consumer Price Index?*

12. Explain the *Fisher equation* and each of its components. Which of the components are generally observed and which are computed?

13. What are some of the measurement problems that arise in quantifying the value of production? List at least five problems with brief explanations of each.

Numerical Questions

1. The table below gives information from the national income accounts for a small country.

Values expressed in current 1998 dollars

Personal consumption expenditures	$1,000	Corporate profits	$200
Gross private domestic investment	250	Dividends	50
Net private domestic investment	220	Net transfer payments	100
Government purchases of goods and services	500		
Net exports	−30	Disposable income	1,585
Imports	50	Proprietors' income	150
Net factor income earned abroad	5	Rent	10
National income	1,685	Interest	140
Interest not in GDP	150		

All information needed to answer the following questions is given in the table. All values not shown there either can be computed from other values in the table (e.g., depreciation and retained earnings) or are assumed to be zero (e.g., business transfers, net surplus of government enterprises, and the statistical discrepancy). Compute values for the following items:

a.   GDP
b.   NDP
c.   Exports
d.   GNP
e.   Indirect business taxes
f.   Retained earnings
g.   Personal income
h.   Individual income taxes
i.   Wages and salaries

2.   Answer each of the following questions based on the incomplete information supplied in the table below.
      a.   Compute nominal GDP in period 1.

Period	Implicit Price Deflator for GDP (period 1 = 100)	Nominal GDP (current $)	Real GDP (period 1 $)
1	100	?	300
2	?	900	600
3	300	1,500	?
4	200	1,200	?

−300

      b.   Compute the price deflator in period 2.
      c.   Compute real GDP in periods 3 and 4.
      d.   Was there a recession in any of the periods? Explain.
      e.   Was there deflation in any of the periods? Explain.

2.   The following table includes price and quantity information on the only two goods produced in an economy. Answer each of the following questions based on that information.

Year	Food Price	Food Quantity	Clothing Price	Clothing Quantity
1998	$30	10	$20	5
1999	$45	20	$25	7

      a.   What are the individual inflation rates for both food and clothing?
      b.   Using 1998 as the base year (for weights and normalization), compute the value of the Consumer Price Index for both years.
      c.   What was the average rate of inflation between 1998 and 1999? Is it the arithmetic average of the two rates in part a above? Why or why not?

d.   Assume that over the same periods your income jumped by 60 percent, from $10,000 to $16,000. Express those values in 1998 dollars and compute the percentage change in your *real* income.

4.   Answer each of the following questions using the table given in question 3, again assuming that food and clothing are the only two goods in the economy.
   a.   Calculate nominal GDP in each year.
   b.   Using 1998 as the base year, calculate real GDP in each year. What was the percent change in real output?
   c.   Compute the GDP deflator for each period and its percentage change between 1998 and 1999. Is this the same as the change in the Consumer Price Index computed in part b of question 3? Why or why not?

5.   Answer each of the following questions regarding the relation of interest rates and inflation.
   a.   Suppose that in 1998 you loaned out $100 at 5 percent interest, to be paid back one year later. Over the year, inflation was 8 percent. Compute the real value, expressed in 1998 dollars, of the money paid back in 1999, as well as the percent change in the real value. (Helpful hint: Use a deflator based in 1998, *not* the Fisher equation.)
   b.   Using the values in part a above and the Fisher equation, compute the real rate of return on the money loaned out. Does it (approximately) equal the percent change in the money's real value, calculated above?
   c.   If you require a real rate of return of 4 percent and the inflation rate is expected to be 3 percent, what interest rate would you charge? Compute the real rate of return if the inflation turns out to be 1 percent, 7 percent, and 10 percent.

Analytical Questions

1.   Which of the following events would be included in this year's gross domestic product?
   a.   You buy a ticket to a Boston Red Sox baseball game.
   b.   You buy a 1960 Mickey Mantle baseball card.
   c.   You buy a Treasury Bill.
   d.   You buy a General Motors corporate bond.
   e.   You buy a new General Motors car that was made in Mexico.
   f.   A Mexican citizen buys a new General Motors car made in Detroit.
   g.   You buy a 1987 Chevrolet.
   h.   You prune the trees in your front yard.
   i.   You hire a tree service to prune the trees in your front yard.

j.   You win a $50 bet with your friend on a football game.

k.   You borrow $100 from your parents.

2. Suppose that you are comparing the standard of living in two countries. One is a developed country with per capita income equal to $17,000 per year; the other is a developing country with per capita income equal to $1,000 per year. Can you conclude that the standard of living in the developed country is 17 times that of the developing country?

3. There has been tremendous concern in the United States about the rapid increase in the price of health care. Indeed, rising medical costs are a major factor in recent calls for an overhaul of the health care system. Despite the great concerns that have been voiced, is there reason to believe that the measured price increases have overstated the true rise in the cost of medical services?

34

PART TWO: FISCAL AND MONETARY POLICY

Chapter 6: Fiscal Policy, Saving, and Growth

Chapter Outline

Introduction

Government expenditures and Finance
        Case study: Postwar U.S. budget deficits

The dynamics of fiscal policy
        The government's intertemporal budget constraint
        Fiscal policy and household behavior
        Case study: U.S. generational accounts

Fiscal policy and economic transitions
        The transition equation with fiscal policy
        Financing government consumption
        Generational policy
        Case study: Explaining the postwar decline in U.S. saving

Deficit finance

Social Security
        The U.S. social security system
        Adding social security to the model
        Case study: Should the United States privatize social security?
        A Caveat: Ricardian equivalence

Government capital formation
        Case study: Government investment in the United States

Intragenerational transfers and distortions
        Intragenerational redistribution: the safety net and its effects
        Distortionary fiscal policy

Chapter summary

Key Terms

    Budget deficit
    Deficit finance
    Distortionary fiscal policy
    Fiscal policy
    Generational account
    Generational policy
    Government intertemporal budget constraint (GIBC)
    Intragenerational redistribution
    Net national debt
    Net taxes
    Pay-as-you-go Social Security
    Primary deficit
    Transfer payments
    Unfunded liability

Key Equations

Net national debt: $B_{t+1} = B_t + D_t$

GIBC: $$B_t + \frac{G_t}{R_t} + \frac{G_{t+1}}{R_t R_{t+1}} + \cdots = \frac{Z_t}{R_t} + \frac{Z_{t+1}}{R_t R_{t+1}} + \cdots$$

Generational account: $$\hat{z}_t = z_{yt} + \frac{z_{ot+1}}{(1+r_{t+1})}$$

Transition equation with fiscal policy ($\alpha = 0$): $k_{t+1} = (1-\beta) A k_t^\beta - f_t$

36

Key Graphs

Transition equation with fiscal policy:

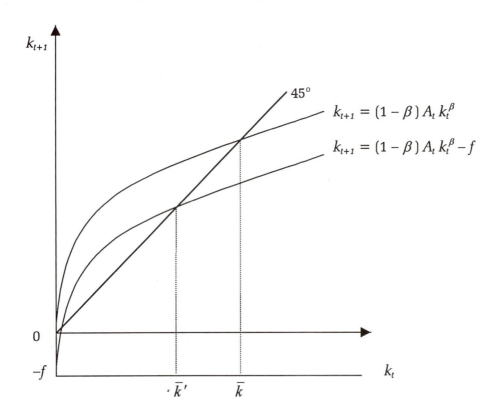

$$k_{t+1} = (1 - \beta) A_t k_t^{\beta}$$

$$k_{t+1} = (1 - \beta) A_t k_t^{\beta} - f$$

QUESTIONS FOR CHAPTER 6

Review Questions

1. What is the *government budget*? What is the *budget deficit*? How has the federal budget deficit behaved in recent decades?

2. Describe the ways in which the government can finance its expenditures.

3. What is the *net national debt*? Write the formula for the stock of government debt. Explain the difference between government expenditures and government purchases of goods and services. What are *net taxes*? Write the formula for the

stock of government debt, including the variables for the components of the budget deficit.

4. Explain the *government intertemporal budget constraint*. Why can it be said that fiscal policy consists of a series of interdependent decisions over time?

5. Explain the "simplified model" adopted in this chapter. That is, even prior to the inclusion of fiscal policy, how is consumption behavior in the two-period life-cycle model modified in the present chapter? How is the household budget constraint modified to include individual net taxes? What is the expression for aggregate tax payments?

6. What is a *generational account*? Which generational account is larger, a one-period tax imposed on the young or the same amount of tax imposed on the same individuals when they are old? Why? What is the typical lifetime pattern of the components of generational accounts?

7. How is the transition equation modified to reflect the simplified consumption decision assumed in this chapter? How is the transition equation modified to include fiscal policy? Explain what is included in the fiscal policy term and why it makes sense for them to be included.

8. Explain the difference between a payroll tax and a consumption tax. In this model, on whom does each fall? What are their effects on the transition equation?

9. What conclusions were reached in the chapter regarding the effect of government consumption on the level of national investment? In particular, does the method of finance matter? Why or why not?

10. What three major programs does the *Social Security system* encompass? Historically, how were Social Security transfer payments financed? Does a $4,000 payroll tax payment when young offset by a $4,000 Social Security benefit when old have any impact on the generational account? Why or why not?

11. What is *Social Security's unfunded liability*? To whom is it an asset and to whom is it a liability?

12. What are examples of *government capital formation*? Write the formula for the transition equation assuming that government capital is added to the nation's

productive capital stock. How does government investment financed by taxes on the young affect the transition path?

13. What is a *distortionary tax* and what implications would such a tax have for the two-period life-cycle model?

14. Under what circumstances will intragenerational transfers (e.g., providing a *safety net* to poorer individuals within the same generation) affect capital formation? What will the effect(s) be?

Numerical Questions

1. Suppose that the government initially has no debt, but suddenly decides to spend $500 each year while collecting only $450 in tax revenue each year. Also suppose that the interest rate, r, is expected to remain at 5 percent for the foreseeable future.
   a. We define the *primary deficit* as government spending minus tax revenue. Compute its value in each of the next four years.
   b. Compute the national debt in each of the next four years.
   c. Compare the growth rate of the national debt to the interest rate. Does the government's fiscal policy satisfy the GIBC? Why or why not?
   d. How might the government change its policy so that the GIBC is satisfied?

2. Suppose that the government enacts a new tax scheme whereby it collects $60 each period from young people and $40 each period from old people. Also, suppose that the interest rate per period, r, is expected to remain at 200 percent for the foreseeable future.
   a. What is the generational account of the old immediately after the tax scheme is implemented?
   b. What is the generational account of the young immediately after the tax scheme is implemented?
   c. Suppose instead that the government collects $100 each period in total, but makes the young pay only $30 each period. What is the generational account of the old immediately after the change? the generational account of the young? Compare your answers to those above.

3. Suppose that output and production are described by Cobb-Douglas functions, and that the following parameter values hold:

Parameter	Value
A	4
α	0
β	0.3
N	100

a. Calculate the steady-state capital-labor ratio and level of output.

b. Suppose that the government decides to purchase 1 unit of output for government consumption each period. To pay for it, the government collects taxes equal to 1 from the old each period. What will the steady-state capital-labor ratio and output level be? Compare these answers to those calculated in part a. Explain any differences or similarities.

c. Now suppose that the government changes its policy and pays for its spending by collecting taxes equal to 1 from the young each period. Calculate the capital-labor ratio and output level for the two periods following the policy change. Compare these answers to the steady-state values calculated in part b. Explain any differences or similarities.

d. Finally, suppose that the government continues to collect taxes equal to 1 from the young each period. Now, however, the government uses the tax revenue to purchase 0.5 unit of capital and 0.5 unit of consumption instead of 1 unit of consumption. What will be the impact of the policy change on the capital-labor ratio and output level in the two periods after the change? Do these differ from the values calculated in part c? Why or why not?

4. Assume that the economy is in a steady state described by the parameters given in question 3. The government embarks on a fiscal policy whereby it purchases 3 units of output each period and finances its spending by collecting taxes of 3 from the young.

a. What values do the capital-labor ratio and interest rate take in the two periods after the change?

b. What is the generational account in the two periods after the change?

c. Suppose again that the economy is in the steady state described by the parameters in question 3. The government then decides to finance spending of 3 each period by borrowing 3 from the young and then taxing the old in the following period by an amount sufficient both to pay back the 3 and to pay interest on the borrowing. What values does the capital-labor ratio take in the two periods following the change? Do they differ from the ratios calculated in part a?

d. What values does the interest rate take in the two periods after the change described in part c, and how much tax will be collected from the old in each period?

5. Assume that the economy is in a steady state described by the parameters given in question 3. Starting today, the government implements a pay-as-you-go tax/transfer program whereby young people pay 2 each period to finance a payment of 2 to each old person. What is the capital-labor ratio and output level in the two periods after the change? How do these values differ from the initial steady-state values? Why?

Analytical Questions

1. If the government imposes a tax on the young to finance government consumption, what happens to saving by the young and the steady-state capital-labor ratio? Now suppose that the elderly care enough about their children to provide them with a gift equal to the amount of the government tax. Relative to the initial steady state (i.e., with no fiscal policy), what will be the effect on the steady-state capital-labor ratio? What will happen to the composition of consumption?

2. The government issues bonds to the young in order to finance a large one-time government consumption expenditure (e.g., for a war). When the bonds come due in the next period, they are reissued to the young at that time in the amount of the initial principal. The interest is obtained by a tax on the elderly at that time. The same procedure is followed in every subsequent period. Explain why this fiscal policy and method of finance satisfy the government intertemporal budget constraint. What is the effect of this fiscal policy on the generational account? Why? What is the effect on the steady-state capital-labor ratio? In what way(s) is this policy similar to a pay-as-you-go Social Security system? In what way(s) is the policy different?

3. Assume the same one-time government consumption expenditure and financing scheme described in question 2. After some number of years, the government repudiates the debt—that is, it unilaterally cancels its obligation to pay back either the principal or the interest due on the national debt. Because it no longer needs to raise revenue to make interest payments, it ceases to tax the elderly. What happens to saving by the young and the steady-state capital-labor ratio? Why don't governments typically adopt such a strategy?

Chapter 7: Money and Prices in the Closed Economy

Chapter Outline

Introduction

What is money?
       Properties of money
       The importance of beliefs and institutions to the definition of money
       Case study: Different monies in U.S. history
       Case study: "Holey Money" is a staple of India's paper currency

The classical view of money
       The quantity equation and velocity
       Is velocity constant?

Adding money to our model
       The lifetime budget constraint with money
       The demand for money
       Case study: Real money balances during the German hyperinflation

Capital accumulation in the monetary economy
       Determination of the price level through time
       A numerical example of a transition with money
       Case study: The U.S. deflation of 1865-1879

When is money neutral?
       Case 1: Printing money to make transfers to the elderly
       Case 2: Printing money to finance government consumption
       Case 3: Printing money to finance transfers to the young

How ongoing increases in the money supply cause inflation
       The inflation process under a more realistic formulation of money demand
       Seigniorage—"the inflation tax"
       Using surprise inflation to reduce the real value of government debt
       Case study: Has the U.S. diluted its debt through unexpected inflation?
       Inflation in the presence of non-indexed government taxation and spending

Chapter summary

42

Key Terms

Bank runs
Barter
Deflation
Demand deposits
Hyperinflation
Liquidity
M1, M2, M3
Monetary policy
Money demand
Neutrality of money
Price level
Quantity equation
Quantity theory of money
Real stock of money
Seigniorage
Velocity of money

Key Equations

Quantity equation:
$$M\,v = P\,Y$$

Lifetime budget constraint with money:
$$\frac{c_{ot+1}}{(1+r_{t+1})} + \frac{i_{t+1}}{(1+i_{t+1})}\frac{m_{t+1}}{P_t} = w_t$$

Utility function w/ money demand:
$$u_t = \left[\frac{m_{t+1}}{P_t}\right]^{\theta} c_{ot+1}^{1-\theta}$$

Demand for real money balances:
$$\frac{m_{t+1}}{P_t} = \gamma\left[i_{t+1}\right]w_t$$

Price level:
$$P_t = \frac{\overline{M}}{\overline{\gamma}w_t N}$$

Transition equation with money:
$$k_{t+1} = (1 - \gamma[i_{t+1}])A(1-\beta)k_t^{\beta} - f_t$$

QUESTIONS FOR CHAPTER 7

Review Questions

1.   What is the *price level*?

2.   What is *money*, and what constitutes the *M1* measure of money?

3.   What does it mean to say that "money is neutral"?

4.   What functions does money perform, and how does the existence of money make economies more efficient?

5.   What is *liquidity*?

6.   What is the *quantity equation,* and how is it used to derive the *quantity theory of money*?

7.   What factors affect the *velocity of money,* and how has the velocity of money in the United States behaved historically?

8.   What is the *opportunity cost* of holding money? How is the *lifetime budget constraint* written when individuals hold money?

9.   How does the life-cycle model incorporate money into the utility function, and what is the resulting equation for the *demand for real money balances*?

10.   How is the *transition equation* written after money is incorporated into the life-cycle model?

11.   How is the *price level* determined in the life-cycle model, and what equation describes its time path? How is the price level affected by a change in the wage? by a change in $\bar{\gamma}$?

12.   Under what circumstances will money be neutral in the life-cycle model? Under what circumstances will money not be neutral?

13.   What is the impact of ongoing increases in the money supply when $\gamma[\ ]$ is constant? when $\gamma[\ ]$ depends on the nominal interest rate?

14. How can money growth and its associated inflation affect the *real fiscal position* of a government?

Numerical Questions

1. Answer each of the following questions based on the data given in the table below.

Year	Real GDP (billions of 1992 chained dollars)	GDP Deflator (1992 = 100)	M1 (billions of dollars)	M2 (billions of dollars)
1970	3397.6	30.5	214.5	628.1
1980	4615.0	60.3	408.8	1,629.5
1990	6136.3	93.6	826.1	3,339.0

For each year, compute the value of each of the following:
   a. The velocity of money using M1. What happens to its value over time?
   b. The velocity of money using M2. What happens to its value over time?
   c. The real money stock using M1.
   d. The real money stock using M2.

2. Suppose an economy is characterized by the following parameters:
   $$\beta = 0.3, A = 5, N = 100, K_o = 200, \overline{M} = 1000, \text{ and } \overline{\gamma} = 0.1$$
   a. For periods 0 through 4, calculate values of the economy's capital-labor ratio, per capita earnings, and the price level.
   b. Compute the steady-state values of the capital-labor ratio, per capita earnings, and the price level.

3. Assume all of the initial values provided in question 2 except the value of $\overline{\gamma}$, which has increased to 0.3.
   a. For periods 0 through 4, calculate values of the economy's capital-labor ratio, per capita earnings, and the price level.
   b. Compute the steady-state values of the capital-labor ratio, per capita earnings, and the price level.
   c. Use a transition diagram to explain why the values for the capital-labor ratio and the real wage in this question differ from their corresponding values in question 2 (i.e., when $\overline{\gamma} = 0.1$).

4. a. Based on the parameter values and steady-state values used for question 3, $(\beta = 0.3, A = 5, N = 100, K_o = 200, \overline{M} = 1000, \text{ and } \overline{\gamma} = 0.3)$, compute the steady-state values of each of the following:
    i.   Real money holdings per person (m/P)
    ii. The real interest rate (r)
    iii. The nominal interest rate (i)
    iv. Consumption by the old (c_o).
    b. Using the steady-state values calculated above, demonstrate that the intertemporal budget constraint is satisfied.

5. With the economy in the steady state calculated in the previous two questions, the government increases the money supply by 500 and gives it to the young.
    a. For periods 0 through 4, calculate values of the economy's capital-labor ratio, per capita earnings, and the price level.
    b. Compute the steady-state values of the capital-labor ratio, per capita earnings, and the price level.
    c. Compare the resulting steady state to the original steady state. Is the policy neutral? Explain.

Analytical Questions

1. Economist Milton Friedman of the University of Chicago once remarked that "Inflation is always and everywhere a monetary phenomenon." Evaluate Friedman's statement. Is ongoing money growth the only way for ongoing inflation to occur, or are there other economic events that could lead to continual increases in the price level?

2. As part of the economic transformation occurring in the countries of the former Soviet Union and Eastern Europe, the banking systems and banking services of those countries are becoming more sophisticated. In many of these countries we see a proliferation of ATMs, credit cards, and debit card arrangements, among other changes. Discuss the economic effects of these developments.

3. Suppose that OPEC suddenly restricts the amount of crude oil that it sells to the United States. Answer the following questions, assuming that γ is constant. (Helpful hint: Think of this as influencing the level of multifactor productivity. Refer to the transition diagram and price level equation when answering.)
    a. What will happen to the price level in the periods after the restriction is imposed?

b. Will the price level in the new steady state be higher than, lower than, or the same as the price level in the initial steady state?

c. Will nominal interest rates in the new steady state be higher than, lower than, or the same as in the initial steady state?

d. Suppose that you are a monetary policy maker and have as your goal price stability. How would you adjust the money supply in light of the restrictions?

4. Suppose that the government has decided to implement a new program whereby transfers are made to the elderly. The government is considering implementing one of two financing options. In the first, the government taxes the young and gives the proceeds to the elderly. In the second, the government simply prints more money to pay for the transfers. Assume, as we did in this chapter, that young people consume nothing and that y is constant. If you are an old person when the policy is announced, which plan will you prefer, and why? If you are a young person when the policy is announced, which plan will you prefer, and why?

PART THREE: ECONOMIC FLUCTUATIONS

Chapter 8: The Keynesian Model of Price and Wage Rigidity

Chapter Outline

Introduction

Price and wage adjustment process
> Fully flexible prices
> Price and wage rigidity
> *Case study:* U.S. magazine prices
> *Case study:* The wage adjustment process
> Price rigidity and the Keynesian model

Developing the Keynesian approach
> Deriving the IS-LM framework
> LM curve
> IS curve

Output determination with rigid prices
> Aggregate demand and unemployment

Influencing output: the role of monetary and fiscal policy
> Monetary policy
> Fiscal policy
> Measuring policy effectiveness

National saving and the paradox of thrift
> *Case study:* Financing social security

Nominal wage rigidity
> Nominal wage rigidity and unemployment
> Aggregate supply curve
> Monetary and fiscal policy in the rigid nominal-wage regime
> Aggregate demand curve

Chapter summary

Key Terms

Aggregate demand curve
Aggregate supply curve
Crowding out
Fiscal policy
Flexible prices
Involuntary unemployment
IS curve
Keynesian model
LM curve
Monetarism
Monetary policy
Multiplier
Nominal rigidity
Paradox of thrift
Potential (full employment) output
Real rigidity
Rigid prices
Voluntary unemployment

Key Equations

LM curve:

$$Y = \frac{M}{\gamma[r_{+1}](1-\beta)\overline{P}}$$

IS curve:

$$Y = \frac{F + \phi[r_{+1}]}{(1-\beta)(1-\gamma[r_{+1}])}$$

Key Graphs

IS-LM graph:

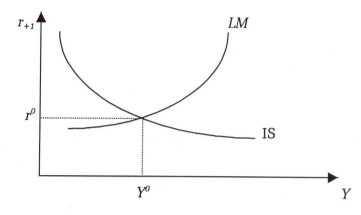

Labor market graph:

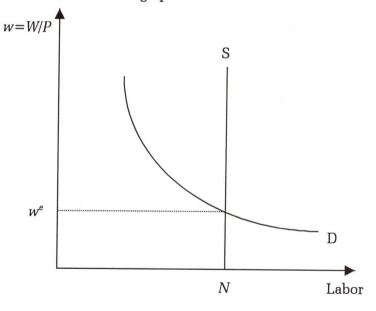

AS/AD graph:

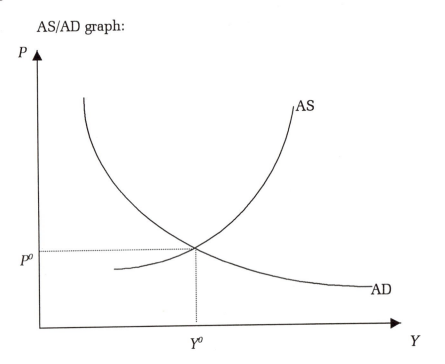

Table 8.1 Impact of Monetary and Fiscal Policy with Rigid Prices: A Summary

Variable	Monetary Policy (Increase in M)	Fiscal Policy (Increase in F)
Output (Y)	Increases	Increases
Employment (L)	Increases	Increases
Consumption (C)	Increases	Increases
Investment (I)	Increases	Decreases
Interest rate, next period (r_{+1})	Decreases	Increases

QUESTIONS FOR CHAPTER 8

Review Questions

1. What is meant by *fully flexible prices*? Provide several examples of markets with fully flexible prices. What properties or conditions in those markets lead to price flexibility?

2. What is meant by *nominal rigidity*? Provide several examples of prices that exhibit nominal rigidity. What conditions lead to such stickiness? Is the stickiness symmetric? Explain.

3. What is meant by *real rigidity*? If the minimum wage were "indexed" to the Consumer Price Index so that it moved equiproportionally in both directions, would this constitute nominal or real wage rigidity? Explain.

4. What have Keynesians traditionally believed about the flexibility of prices and wages in the short run versus the long run? How can this assumption of price adjustment be incorporated into the life-cycle model?

5. Write the equation for the *LM curve*. What values are constant in the LM equation? What is the nature of the relationship captured by the LM curve?

6. Write the equation for the *IS curve*. What values are constant in the IS equation? What is the nature of the relationship captured by the IS curve?

7. What is *involuntary* (or *Keynesian*) *unemployment*, and how does it arise?

8. What is *monetary policy*, and what effect does it have on the position of the LM curve? What is the *multiplier process*, and how does it arise in response to an increase in the money stock? Why might the ultimate rise in output following a monetary expansion be smaller than the magnitude of the LM curve's shift?

9. What is *fiscal policy*, and what effect does it have on the position of the IS curve? Explain the nature of *crowding out* and how it helps determine the initial and ultimate effects of fiscal policy on both output and investment.

10. In the *short run*, what are the common and differing effects of monetary and fiscal policy? In the *long run*, what differences exist between the use of monetary and fiscal policy? Why?

11. What is *monetarism*, and what belief do monetarists hold regarding the interest sensitivity of money demand?

12. How is the effectiveness of monetary policy related to the interest sensitivity of money demand? Why? How is the effectiveness of fiscal policy related to the interest sensitivity of money demand? Why?

13. What is a policy *multiplier*, and how is it measured? What is the monetary policy multiplier if the IS curve is horizontal? Why?

14. What is the *paradox of thrift*, and why is it considered a paradox?

15. Are all increases in national saving associated with reductions in output, according to the Keynesian model? Why or why not?

16. Why does involuntary unemployment arise under *nominal wage rigidity* with price flexibility?

17. Why is the stimulative effect of fiscal and monetary policy on output smaller under nominal wage rigidity with price flexibility than it is under price rigidity? How is this difference show graphically?

18. What are the determinants of the *aggregate demand* curve? What are the determinants of the *aggregate supply* curve? How would expansionary fiscal or monetary policy affect this model?

Numerical Questions

Use the following initial parameter values for questions 1 through 5. Change the values only when indicated.

Parameter	Value
N	200
A	4
β	0.3
$\overline{P}$	1
$\overline{M}$	297.5
F	0

Also, let the parameters γ and ϕ be related to the real interest rate, r_{+1}, by the equations:

$$\gamma[r_{+1}] = 0.727188 - 0.25\ r_{+1}$$

$$\phi[r_{+1}] = 260/r_{+1}$$

1. a. Calculate the values of r_{+1} that lie along the LM curve and correspond to the given levels of output. Also, calculate the value of γ for each of the computed r_{+1}.

Y	r_{+1}	γ
750		
800		
850		
900		
950		

b. Suppose that the government now decides to increase $\overline{M}$ by 10. Calculate the new level of Y for each of the r_{+1} computed in part a. Has the LM schedule shifted to the right or to the left?

c. Suppose that $\overline{M}$ is back to its initial level, but that money demand becomes more sensitive to interest rate changes. Specifically, assume that the coefficient on r_{+1} in the equation describing γ is -0.5, not -0.25. Calculate the new values of r_{+1} that lie along the LM schedule and correspond to the levels of output given in part a.

Y	r_{+1}
750	
800	
850	
900	
950	

Compare your answers to those calculated in part a. Has the increased interest sensitivity of money demand made the LM schedule steeper or flatter? Explain.

2.   a.   Using the initial parameter values, calculate the values of r_{+1} that lie along the IS curve and correspond to the given levels of output. In doing so, assume for this problem that γ is *constant* and equal to 0.5.

Y	r_{+1}
750	
800	
850	
900	
950	

    b.   Suppose that the government decides to increase F from 0 to 10. Calculate the new levels of output that correspond to the values of r_{+1} computed in part a. Has the IS schedule shifted to the right or to the left?

    c.   Suppose that F once again equals 0, but that the value of γ falls from 0.5 to 0.3. Recalculate the values of r_{+1} for the levels of output given in part a. What does the change in γ do to the position of the IS curve? Give the economic intuition behind the change.

3.   Suppose that the initial parameter values hold, but that the Federal Reserve has as its goal to keep the interest rate at 0.908785. That is, the Fed will change the money supply by whatever it takes to keep interest rates constant at 0.908785.

    a.   What is the equilibrium output level under these circumstances? (Helpful hint: Since the Fed will shift the LM curve as much as necessary, you need to find the correct point on the IS curve as in question 2. Continue to assume that $\gamma = 0.5$.)

    b.   If the government increases F from 0 to 10, by how much will equilibrium output change?

    c.   When F increases by 10, by how much must M change to keep interest rates unchanged?

4.   Suppose, as a monetarist would, that the value of γ is constant and equal to 0.5 both for the LM schedule and for the IS schedule. Using the initial values, answer parts a through d.

    a.   What are the fixed-price equilibrium levels of Y and r_{+1}? (Helpful hint: Set the IS curve and LM curve equal.)

    b.   Using the same parameter values, now assume that prices are *flexible*. What are the flexible price equilibrium values of Y and r_{+1}?

    c.   Based on your answers to parts a and b, is there unemployment in part a? Why?

d.   Compute the flexible price equilibrium *price level*. How does this value compare to the initially fixed price level? Is the difference consistent with your answer to part c?

Analytical Questions

1.   Suppose that the economy is characterized by price rigidity and is presently below full employment. In order to raise the level of current output, the government increases its consumption purchases and finances them by taking resources from the young. You are an economist for the Federal Reserve Board, and the Chair asks you to devise a way to exactly offset any crowding out that might result from the fiscal policy. What would you propose, and what would be the ultimate effect of your plan (in conjunction with the fiscal policy) on the interest rate? on the level of output? on the composition of output? Explain.

2.   Social upheaval erupts and leads to the theft and burning of large quantities of money. Trace the effects on an economy characterized by price rigidity. In particular, what would happen to the economy's interest rate, the level of current output, and the composition of output? What would be the effect, if any, on the nation's future productive capacity? Explain.

3.   The economy is currently below full employment. There is a binding minimum wage rate, though prices are flexible.
   a.   The Labor Secretary asks Congress to raise the minimum wage rate. What would happen to output, the interest rate, and capital formation?
   b.   The Labor Secretary loses the battle for an increased minimum wage as a result of successful lobbying efforts by the American Association of Manufacturers, which manages to get Congress to eliminate the minimum wage. What will happen to the nominal wage rate, the real wage rate, current output, and capital formation? Explain how these changes would affect future adjustments in the economy.

Chapter 9: Understanding Recessions

Chapter Outline

Introduction

The 1950-1969 Phillips curve and the Keynesian model
    Shifting Phillips curve

Natural rate hypothesis
    Is the natural rate of unemployment positive?
    The Phillips curve and the traditional Keynesian model: a summary

The short-run trade-off versus rational expectations

Misperception theory
    Illustrating a misperception model with a labor supply and demand diagram
    Case study: International comparisons of the inflation-unemployment trade-off
    Critiquing the misperception theory

Real business cycle theory
    Illustrating a real business cycle
    Generating different business cycles by varying the assumed path of A
    How do real business cycle models explain unemployment?
    How well do real business cycle models explain the business cycle?
    Critiquing the real business cycle model
    Case study: Oil price shocks and recessions

Sectoral shift model
    Critiquing the sectoral shift model
    Policies to deal with sectoral shifts

New Keynesian models of recessions
    Long-term nominal wage and price contracts
    Other explanations of nominal rigidities
    Case study: Do anticipated or unanticipated money shocks affect U.S. output?
    Coordination failures
        Coordination failures and recessions
        Illustrating coordination failures with our model
        Case study: Consumer and business confidence and the business cycle

Policy responses to coordination failures
Political business cycles

What causes recessions? A bottom line

Chapter summary

Key Terms

Coordination failure
Frictional unemployment
Intertemporal substitution
Job vacancy rate
Menu costs
Misperceptions theory
Multiple equilibria
Natural rate of unemployment
New Keynesian models
Phillips curve
Political business cycle theory
Rational expectations
Real business cycle theory
Sectoral shift model
Staggered contracts

Table 9.3 Alternative Explanations of Recessions and Their Policy Implications

Theory	Cause of Recession	Policy Implications
Traditional Keynesian, Model	Nominal wage or price rigidities prevent the economy from equilibrating at full employment.	Monetary or fiscal policy can be used to expand output.
Misperception Theory	Workers (firms) misconstrue decreases in their nominal wages (prices) arising from unexpected decreases in the money supply as reductions in their real wages (prices); they reduce their supply of (demand for) labor; output falls.	Workers and firms have rational expectations, so only unexpected changes in the money supply have real effects.
Real Business Cycle Theory	Workers voluntarily work less during periods when their real wages are low. Temporarily low real wages reflect negative technology shocks.	Since unemployment is voluntary, there is no economic rationale for policy intervention.
Sectoral Shift Model	Shocks to particular sectors of the economy lead to time-consuming reallocation of inputs across sectors; this reallocation temporarily lowers output.	Government assistance in helping labor and capital relocate may mitigate output loss.
New Keynesian Theories of Wage and Price Rigidities	Explicit or implicit long-term contracts, inertia, imperfect competition, or menu costs explain nominal wage and price rigidities that prevent the economy from reaching full employment	Depending on the source of the nominal rigidity, expected as well as unexpected increases in the money supply can raise output.
New Keynesian Models of Coordination Failures	Failure of firms to coordinate actions (e.g., searching for one another or setting the same operating hours) leads to low output equilibrium.	Government pep talks may help the private sector choose high output equilibrium.
Political Business Cycles	Incumbent politicians expand economy prior to elections; once they are reelected, they contract the economy.	Monetary and fiscal policies are used for short-term political expediency. Independence of fiscal and monetary authorities from politicians can help.

QUESTIONS FOR CHAPTER 9

Review Questions

1.   What empirical relationship does the *Phillips curve* describe? How has the Phillips curve actually changed over the last 40 to 50 years?

2.   How is the Phillips curve explained by the *traditional Keynesian model*? According to this model, what can government policy do to reduce unemployment during recessions?

3.   What is the *natural rate of unemployment*? Is a natural rate of unemployment of zero a realistic possibility?

4.   How are *rational expectations* about inflation formed? How do rational expectations affect the government's ability to change the unemployment rate? How can a Phillips curve arise if expectations about inflation are formed rationally?

5.   What is the *misperceptions theory* of the Phillips curve? According to this theory, what can government policy do to reduce unemployment during recessions?

6.   What criticisms have been raised against the misperceptions model? How have proponents of the model answered these criticisms?

7.   How does the *real business cycle theory* explain recessions? What kinds of economic shocks are encompassed by the theory? How does the real business cycle theory explain unemployment? According to this theory, what can government policy do to reduce unemployment during recession?

8.   What criticisms have been raised against the real business cycle model? How have proponents of the model answered these criticisms?

9.   How does the *sectoral shift model* explain recessions? What events can initiate sectoral shifts? According to this model, what can government policy do to reduce unemployment during recessions?

10.   What criticisms have been raised against the sectoral shift model? How have proponents of the model answered these criticisms?

11. Describe the ways in which *New Keynesians* have modeled nominal wage and price rigidity.

12. Describe empirical evidence that has examined whether *anticipated* monetary policy changes affect output.

13. What are *coordination failures*, and what two elements are common to almost all models of coordination failure? How do models of coordination failure explain business cycles? According to these models, what can government policy do to reduce unemployment during recessions?

14. How does the theory of *political business cycles* explain the economy's cyclical fluctuations? How might this theory operate in the context of a traditional Keynesian model? in the context of the real business cycle model?

Numerical Questions

1. Assume that the economy is characterized by the two-period life-cycle model as presented in Chapter 4, in which the young save a portion of their income, α, but not all of it. In particular, assume the following parameter values: $\alpha = 0.5$, $\beta = 0.3$, $N = 200$, and $K_o = 462.4$.
    a. Assuming that $A_t = 5$ for all t, what are the steady-state values of the capital-labor ratio (k), individual earnings (w), the interest rate (r), aggregate output (Y), and aggregate consumption (C)?
    b. Instead of the single value of A_t, assume that $A_o = 4$, $A_1 = 5$, and $A_2 = 6$, and that the pattern repeats beginning in period 3 (and again in periods 6, 9, etc.). Use $K_o = 462.4$. As in Table 9.1 in the text, use a spreadsheet program to compute the value of the following for 12 periods after the initial period: the capital-labor ratio (k_t), individual earnings (w_t), the interest rate (r_t), aggregate output (Y_t), aggregate savings (S_t), and aggregate consumption (C_t).

2. Based on the model specified in question 1, answer the following questions regarding economic fluctuations resulting from technology shocks.
    a. In the long run, what is the percentage drop in A_t from its maximum value to its minimum value? What is the corresponding drop in output in the long run as A_t drops? Explain how the changes in the capital-labor ratio over the model's business cycle dampen somewhat the impact of the changes in technology on output.

b.   Compare percentage changes in aggregate output and aggregate consumption, and comment on the following statement: "In addition to dampening output fluctuations, the volatile pattern of saving serves to stabilize consumption." Is consumption more or less volatile than output? Is this view consistent with the Chapter 4 discussion of consumption smoothing?

3.   Suppose the Phillips curve is given by the equation $u = 6 - 0.5(\pi - \pi^e)$, where u is the rate of unemployment, π is the rate of inflation, and π^e is the expected rate of inflation.

a.   Assume that the expected rate of inflation is 3 percent. Calculate the rate of unemployment for values of inflation between 0 and 17 percent.
b.   What is the value of the natural rate of unemployment?
c.   Assume that the expected rate of inflation rises to 7 percent. Recalculate the unemployment rate associated with inflation rates ranging from 0 to 17 percent.
d.   With the unemployment rate on the horizontal axis, plot values of actual inflation associated with unemployment rates ranging from 1 to 7.5 (by half points). What has happened to the Phillips curve with changed inflationary expectations?

Analytical Questions

1.   Suppose that the government substantially reduces military spending.
a.   Analyze the likely effects of the spending cut on output, employment, and unemployment using (1) the traditional Keynesian model; (2) the sectoral shift model; and (3) the real business cycle model.
b.   How could you use your answers to part a to assess the empirical validity of the alternative theories?

2.   In some New Keynesian models, the frequency with which firms change prices depends explicitly on the inflation rate. Would you expect a direct relationship between the level of inflation and the frequency of price change or an inverse relationship, and why?

3.   Suppose that past and current monetary growth has led to persistent inflation. Policy makers suddenly announce that money growth will be reversed so that prices will return to their levels of three years ago. Once that goal is achieved, money will then grow at a rate consistent with price stability. Does the misperception model offer a clear prediction about the impact of this policy

change on the level of output? If it does, on what does the predicted impact depend?

Chapter 10: The Nature and Costs of Unemployment

Chapter Outline

Introduction

Labor force dynamics
      Net versus gross changes in work status
      Case study: Small business—the engine of job creation?
      The sources and duration of unemployment

Labor force dynamics and theories of unemployment
      Involuntary unemployment
          Models of real wage rigidity
          Case study: Wages in the fast-food industry
      Voluntary unemployment
      Misperception unemployment
      Frictional unemployment
      Summary

Unemployment: a disaggregate view
      Differences by sex in employment and unemployment
      Unemployment distinctions by age and race
      Spells of unemployment: the long and the short

Private and social costs of unemployment
      Unemployment and welfare
          Does reduced output overstate the costs of unemployment?
          Does reduced output understate the costs of unemployment?
      Spreading the burden of unemployment: unemployment insurance
          Case study: Does unemployment insurance cause unemployment?

Benefits of reducing unemployment: Okun's Law and the natural rate
      Okun's Law
      Determining the natural rate of unemployment
      Case study: Unemployment in the United States and Europe

Summing up: unemployment and what to do about it

Chapter summary

64

Key Terms

Discouraged workers
Disguised unemployment
Duration of unemployment
Efficiency wage theory
Home production
Hysteresis
Insider-outsider theory
Labor force participation rate
Labor hoarding
Layoffs
Natural rate of unemployment
New hires
Okun's Law
Quits
Rehires

Key Equations

Growth rate of labor input:

$$\frac{\Delta L}{L} = \frac{\Delta H}{H} + \frac{\Delta LF}{LF} - \Delta u$$

Key Graphs

Labor market with efficiency wage and unemployment:

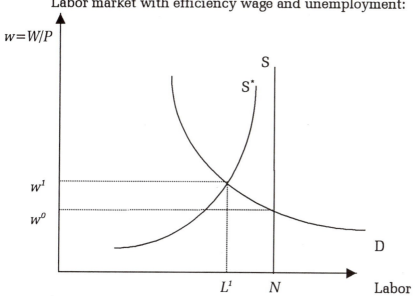

Table 10.1 Theories of Unemployment: Causes, Evidence, Costs, and Policy Responses

Type of Unemployment	Cyclical	Long-Term
Involuntary		
Cause	Nominal rigidity	Real rigidity (insider-outsider, efficiency wage)
Evidence	Layoffs rise in recession	Efficiency wage patterns observed
Costs	Lost output in excess of value of leisure	Lost output in excess of value of leisure
Policy	Expansionary policy	Expansionary policy, if natural rate can be influenced (hysteresis)
Voluntary		
Cause	Fluctuations in real wages or value of leisure	Leisure more valuable than output
Evidence	Unemployment is sensitive to the receipt of unemployment compensation	Quits lead to a stable share of unemployment
Costs	None (negative, since being unemployed is a voluntary decision)	None (negative, since being unemployed is a voluntary decision)
Policy	None	None
Frictional		
Cause	Sectoral shifts	Job search and labor turnover
Evidence	Unemployment rate higher during periods of greater industrial transition	Much unemployment comes in short spells
Costs	None (part of normal labor market process)	None (part of normal labor market process)
Policy	None	None

QUESTIONS FOR CHAPTER 10

Review Questions

1. What is meant by *labor force dynamics*, and what are the three labor market states a person can be in?

2. What is the *labor force participation rate*? What is a *discouraged worker*, and in what way does the existence of discouraged workers explain the cyclical pattern of the labor force participation rate?

3. What terms describe *transitions* into employment and transitions out of employment? Identify the two categories into which each of these types of transitions can be divided.

4. In general terms, what are *gross flows* and *net flows*? Explain the labor force dynamics that are operating when net flows to employment are negative.

5. Explain the following statement: "The net flows indicate the direction of movement of the economy as a whole, whereas the gross flows indicate how much mobility there is in the labor force."

6. "Small business is the 'engine' of job creation." Use your knowledge of both net and gross flows to comment on the validity of this statement.

7. What are the three initial reasons for unemployment? Which is the major source of the volatility of unemployment? Which of the reasons is most consistent with the Keynesian view?

8. How is the *duration* of unemployment typically measured, and how does the duration of unemployment change during recessions? How is *long-term* unemployment generally defined?

9. What is *insider-outsider theory*, and how does it contribute to an explanation of unemployment?

10. What is *efficiency wage theory*, and how does it contribute to an explanation of unemployment?

11. What type of employment separation is consistent with the notion of *voluntary unemployment* and how does this vary over recessions and booms?

12. What is the nature of *frictional unemployment*, and what happens to frictional unemployment during recessions? What would the sectoral shift model predict about the variation of frictional employment during recessions? Why?

13. Since 1950, what has happened to the labor force participation rates of women and men? How have their relative unemployment rates changed over the same period of time? What demographic groups have experienced both higher levels and more volatile swings in unemployment?

14. What are the *private costs* and the *social costs* of unemployment? In what ways does reduced output overstate and understate the costs of unemployment? Why is the cost of voluntary unemployment said to be zero or negative?

15. What mechanism is used to spread the burden of unemployment? Does this mechanism eliminate the costs of unemployment?

16. What is *Okun's Law*? What insights about the nature of this relationship are gained by using the growth accounting framework?

17. What is the *natural rate of unemployment* and, approximately, what is its current value? What has happened to its estimated value over time? Why?

18. What is meant by *hysteresis*? What implications does this theory have for policy?

Numerical Questions

1. Answer parts a through d using the information in the table below.

Year	New Hires	Layoffs	Quits	Rehires	Net Entrants to Labor Force
1	100	80	12	8	20
2	95	85	11	6	25
3	90	90	9	3	30
4	98	85	10	5	35

a. Calculate the gross accessions in each of the four years.
b. Calculate the gross separations in each of the four years.
c. Calculate the change in employment in each of the four years.
d. Calculate the change in unemployment in each of the four years.

2. Suppose that there are 50 people in the labor force and that 13 people experience a spell of unemployment during a particular year. Twelve of the 13 without jobs are unemployed for only one month during the year, but each is unemployed in a different month—the first in January, the second in February, etc. The thirteenth jobless person is unemployed for all 12 months of the year. Finally, suppose that the government measures unemployment monthly.

    a. What is the unemployment rate in each month during the year?
    b. What fraction of unemployment in a given month is made up of short-term unemployment? of long-term unemployment? Compare your answers to the proportion of people unemployed for one month versus one year during the year as a whole. Explain any difference.
    c. Suppose that the people who experience unemployment during the year are cloned, so that there are now two of each for a total of 26 out of a total labor force of 63. What effect does the increase in the number of unemployed people have on the unemployment rate in each month?
    d. Suppose that the initial situation once again holds. Now assume that each person who was unemployed for one month instead is unemployed for two months at a time—the first person in December and January, the second in January and February, etc. What effect does the increased duration of unemployment have on the unemployment rate each month?

3. Using Okun's Law, as illustrated in Figure 10.12 in the text, complete the following table.

Change in Unemployment Rate	Percentage Change in Real GDP
0.05	
−0.02	
−0.01	
0.03	

Analytical Questions

1. According to the "shirking" model of the efficiency wage theory, employers pay a wage above the market-clearing level as a deterrent to shirking. Does the possibility of losing an above-market wage itself actually lead workers to shirk less?

2.	Empirical evidence discussed in the chapter suggests that the unemployment insurance program actually leads to more unemployment. Is the additional unemployment necessarily bad? Is there a sense in which any resulting unemployment might actually help the economy over the long run?

3.	How would the following events affect Okun's Law? (Helpful hint: you may want to think about this question in terms of the growth accounting equation.)
	a.	A decrease in productivity growth
	b.	A greater tendency of workers to leave the labor force during recessions and reenter during expansions
	c.	A rise in β in the Cobb-Douglas production function.

Chapter 11: Countercyclical Policy

Chapter Outline

Introduction

Assessing the costs and benefits of intervention
    The costs of inflation
    The costs of anticipated inflation
    What is the right comparison
    Summary

Monetary and fiscal policy during the Great Depression
    Case study: Monetary policy and the onset of the Depression
    Case study: The slow recovery and the role of policy

The challenge of activist policy
    Policy lags
    Case study: The 1992 presidential election and the recession
    Lags and the determination of policy
    Imperfect information
    Case study: "Whip Inflation Now" and the oil shock
    Rational expectations and the Lucas critique
    Dynamic inconsistency

Additional tools to fight inflation: wage and price controls and incomes policies
    Case study: Nixon's wage-price freeze

What has policy achieved?

Chapter summary

Key Terms

    Automatic stabilizers
    Dynamic inconsistency
    Full employment deficit
    Incomes policy
    Inside lag

72

Lucas critique
Outside lag
Policy lag
Precommitment strategy
Stagflation
Wage and price controls

QUESTIONS FOR CHAPTER 11

Review Questions

1. The text states that when comparing the costs of higher inflation with the benefits of lower unemployment, the question of how permanent the changes are is probably more important than refinements to the measured annual costs of inflation and employment. Explain this statement.

2. What was the path of output during the 1930s?

3. What evidence exists that changes in the money supply contributed to the Great Depression? Are changes in the money supply the only driving forces in the Great Depression? Identify alternative possible causes of the Great Depression.

4. Why is it difficult to measure the *stance of fiscal policy*? What measure has been constructed to overcome the problem?

5. What types of *lags* are involved in the policy process?

6. What sorts of *uncertainties* do policy makers face?

7. What is the *Lucas critique*?

8. What is a *dynamically inconsistent* policy? How can a *precommitment strategy* help overcome the problem of dynamic inconsistency?

9. What are *wage and price controls*? What problems can wage and price controls cause?

10. What are *incomes policies*? How can these policies be used to improve the inflation-unemployment trade-off faced by policy makers?

Analytical Questions

1. In their original article on dynamic inconsistency, Finn Kydland and Edward Prescott discuss government patent policy. The government's goals are to encourage innovation and to make innovations available to a wide array of firms. To accomplish this goal, the government grants patents on innovations, which guarantee that all proceeds from the innovation accrue to the inventing firm for some period of time. Kydland and Prescott claim that such a policy is dynamically inconsistent. In what sense is the policy dynamically inconsistent? How might the problems associated with this policy's dynamic inconsistency be mitigated?

2. "The introduction of wage and price controls is likely to give rise to a black market for various goods and services." Explain.

3. Suppose that someone claimed that a recently observed increase in real output was due to an increase in the money supply. What kinds of data patterns would you look for to corroborate or disprove the claim?

PART FOUR: THE INTERNATIONAL ECONOMY

Chapter 12: Saving and Growth in the International Economy

Chapter Outline

Introduction

International investment and the trade deficit
       Factor price equalization
       Evidence on factor price equalization

Analyzing the two-country model
       Worldwide transition equation
       Asset accumulation along the transition path
       Tracing the world economy's transition
       Net foreign investment during the transition
       The trade balance during the transition
       A transition arising from a decline in the U.S. propensity to save
       Case study: U.S. trade deficits and saving in the 1980s

Effects of trade policy
       The costs of restricting foreign investment
       Recovering from a war with and without foreign investment
       Case study: Japan after World War II
       Case study: U.S. industrialization in the nineteenth century
       Fiscal policy in the open economy

Chapter summary

Appendix 12A: Tracing the path of the world economy

Key Terms

       Autarky
       Domestic investment
       Exports
       Factor price equalization

Gains from trade
Imports
Net foreign asset position
Net foreign investment
Trade deficit

Key Equations

World capital-labor ratio:

$$k_{t+1} = \frac{Na_{t+1} + Na_{t+1}^*}{N + N^*}$$

World transition equation:

$$k_{t+1} = (1 - \overline{\alpha})(1 - \beta)Ak_t^\beta$$

$$\overline{\alpha} = \frac{N\alpha + N^*\alpha^*}{N + N^*}$$

World transition equation
with fiscal policy:

$$k_{t+1} = (1 - \overline{\alpha})(1 - \beta)Ak_t^\beta - \bar{f}$$

$$\bar{f} = \frac{Nf + N^*f^*}{N + N^*}$$

Key Graphs

Two country equilibrium:

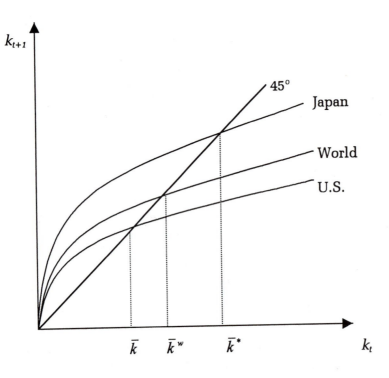

Appendix 12A Tracing the Path of the World Economy

1. Wages and interest rates are based on the world capital-labor ratio:

$$w_t = (1-\beta)A_t k_t^{\beta} \qquad r_t = \beta A_t k_t^{(\beta-1)}$$

2. Domestic assets per old person equal last period's saving by the young:

$$a_t = (1-\alpha)w_{t-1}$$

3. Calculate consumption by the young and old:

$$c_{yt} = \alpha w_t \qquad\qquad c_{ot} = a_t(1+r_t)$$

4. National saving equals national income less consumption:

$$S_t = Nw_t + r_t Na_t - Nc_{yt} - Nc_{ot}$$

5. The world capital stock evolves according to:

$$k_{t+1} = (1-\overline{\alpha})(1-\beta)A_t k_t^{\beta}$$

6. Domestic investment is the change in domestic capital; net foreign investment is the difference between national saving and domestic investment:

$$I_t = Nk_{t+1} - Nk_t \qquad I_t^f = S_t - I_t$$

7. Net foreign assets equal domestic assets less domestic capital; net exports equal net foreign investment less net foreign capital income:

$$K_t^f = Na_t - Nk_t \qquad X_t - M_t = I_t^f - r_t K_t^f$$

QUESTIONS FOR CHAPTER 12

Review Questions

1. What is a *trade deficit*?

2. What is *net foreign investment*? Explain two ways that a country can invest internationally.

3. How is the common, world-wide capital-labor ratio at any point in time expressed in variables?

4. Suppose that there are only two countries that are alike except for their time preference parameter, α. How is the world-wide transition equation written and what value will the world-wide α have? What if the two countries are even the same size?

5. Where does the asset curve of a country with a high saving propensity lie in relation to that of a country with a low saving propensity? Where does the world-wide transition curve lie in relation to the curves for the individual countries?

6. What is *factor price equalization* and what is the mechanism by which it occurs? Does empirical evidence support the idea of factor price equalization?

7. What is a country's *net foreign asset position* and how is it shown in a transition diagram?

8. How does the net foreign asset position of a low-saving country change as the country moves from autarky to free trade?

9. How does the trade balance of a low-saving country change as the country moves from autarky to free trade?

10. Who wins and who loses as a result of *trade restrictions*?

11. Why do trade restrictions reduce world consumption?

12. How is the open-economy model modified to show each country's *fiscal policy*?

Numerical Questions

Suppose that the world consists of only two countries, Savum and Spendum. The following values apply to the Cobb-Douglas production functions and utility functions of each country. Use these values to answer questions 1 through 3 about each country's *steady state*.

Parameter	Savum	Spendum
A	4	4
α	0.3	0.6
β	0.25	0.25
N	100	200

1.   a.   Calculate the steady-state values of k, w, and r for each country under autarky.
       b.   Compare the steady-state values calculated in part a. Do the differences make economic sense?
       c.   Calculate the world-wide value of α.
       d.   Calculate the steady-state values of k, w, and r for each country under free trade.
       e.   Compare Savum's steady-state values under autarky to those under free trade. Explain any differences.

2.   Answer the following questions for the steady state:
       a.   What are the net foreign asset positions of Savum and Spendum in autarky?
       b.   Calculate the total capital stocks of Savum and Spendum under free trade.
       c.   Calculate the total amounts of assets owned by Savum and Spendum under free trade.
       d.   What are the total net foreign asset positions of Savum and Spendum under free trade?
       e.   Does the net foreign asset position of each country under autarky versus free trade make economic sense in terms of the countries' behavioral differences?

3.   a.   What are the steady-state net foreign incomes of Savum and Spendum under autarky?
       b.   What are the steady-state trade balances for each country under autarky?

    c.   What are the steady-state net foreign incomes of Savum and Spendum under free trade?

    d.   What are the steady-state trade balances for each country under free trade?

4.   a.   Calculate the steady-state levels of consumption per person for old people and young people in each country under autarky.

          b.   Calculate the steady-state utility of each young person in each country under autarky.

          c.   Calculate the steady-state levels of consumption per person for old people and young people in each country under free trade. Compare them to the values under autarky and explain any differences.

          d.   Calculate the steady-state utility of each young person in each country under free trade. Compare this to the utility value under autarky and explain any differences.

Analytical Questions

1.   Suppose that Savum and Spendum are in steady-state positions under free trade based on the parameters given in the table in the previous section. Suddenly, Spendum's value of α falls to 0.25. Give *qualitative* answers to the following questions, using transition diagrams to aid your reasoning.

          a.   What is the impact on the capital-labor ratios in Savum and Spendum in the period following the change? on the world-wide capital-labor ratio?

          b.   What is the impact on interest rates and capital flows in each country in the period following the change?

          c.   In the new steady state, which country will be a net debtor? a net creditor?

          d.   In the new steady-state, which country has a trade surplus? a trade deficit?

2.   Suppose that a developed country with a high saving propensity were to donate part of its capital stock to a low-saving, underdeveloped country. Assume that neither technology nor the size of the labor force in each country changes. Analyze whether the donation of capital stock would raise the standard of living in the underdeveloped country either temporarily or permanently. Does your answer depend on whether the donation occurs under autarky or free trade? (Helpful hint: Use transition diagrams to help your reasoning.)

3.   Suppose that the United States and Japan are in steady-state equilibrium under autarky, as pictured in Figure 12.2 in the text. Assume that all trade restrictions are lifted and that *both labor and capital are mobile*, although the total amount of labor is fixed.

a.   What will the capital and labor flows look like as the countries move to the new free-trade, steady-state position? (Helpful hint: What happens to the relative interest rates *and* wages after the change, and how are labor and capital likely to respond?)

b.   Will the steady-state capital-labor ratio be different from the ratio that prevails when labor is not mobile? What about the steady-state wage and interest rate?

c.   Will the steady-state net foreign asset position and steady-state trade balance of each country be different from those that prevail when labor is not mobile?

Chapter 13: Money, Exchange Rates, and Policy in the Open Economy

Chapter Outline

Introduction

Understanding exchange rates
  Case study: Postwar U.S. exchange rate regimes
  Case study: Fixed exchange rates under the gold standard

The law of one price and real versus nominal exchange rates
  Case study: Purchasing power parity and international Big Mac prices
  Real versus nominal exchange rates
  Box 13.1: Big MacCurrencies—Can hamburgers provide hot tips about exchange rates?

Adding another country to our model with money
  Relating the nominal exchange rate to foreign and domestic price levels
  Relating the exchange rate to the money supplies of each country
  Adding the real side to the model
  Determining all real and nominal variables

Managing the exchange rate
  Distinguishing flexible and fixed exchange rate regimes
  Illustrating monetary policy in a flexible exchange rate regime
  Illustrating monetary policy in a fixed exchange rate regime
  Do flexible and fixed exchange rate regimes really differ?
  Case study: Stabilizing the Argentine peso

Arguments for and against flexible and fixed exchange rates
  Transactions costs and flexible exchange rates
  Independence in the operation of monetary policy
  Maintaining a fixed exchange rate with limited international reserves
  Speculation against fixed exchange rate regimes

The open economy model with nominal wage rigidity
  IS curve in the open economy
  Policies in small, open economies with rigid nominal wages
  An argument for fixed exchange rates: mitigating output fluctuations

Case study: European monetary integration
Chapter summary

Key Terms

Appreciation
Arbitrage
Depreciation
Devaluation
Exchange rate
Fixed exchange rates
Flexible exchange rates
Gold standard
International reserves
Law of one price
Nominal exchange rate
Purchasing power parity
Real exchange rate
Revaluation

Key Equations

Real exchange rate:

$$e^R = \frac{P}{P^* / e}$$

Relationship between nominal exchange rate and foreign and domestic inflation rates:

$$\frac{e_{t+1} - e_t}{e_t} = \pi^*_{t+1} - \pi_{t+1}$$

Relating the exchange rate and the money supplies:

$$e = \frac{M^* / N^*}{M / N}$$

QUESTIONS FOR CHAPTER 13

Review Questions

1. What is an *exchange rate*? How is it measured? Compare the exchange rate between the U.S. and France as viewed by each country.

2. What is meant by the *appreciation* and *depreciation* of a country's currency?

3. How are exchange rates determined under a *flexible exchange rate system*? How are they determined under a *fixed exchange rate system*?

4. What is meant by the terms *devaluation* and *revaluation*? How do these adjustments occur?

5. In what ways can a government fix its exchange rate? What is an *overvalued* and an *undervalued* currency?

6. What is a *commodity standard*, and what is the effect of two countries' adopting the same standard? What commodity has been used in this way?

7. Explain the concept of *arbitrage* and its relevance to the *law of one price*. What factors must be considered in determining whether an arbitrage opportunity exists or whether the law of one price holds? What is *purchasing power parity*?

8. Distinguish between the *nominal exchange rate* and the *real exchange rate*. What is meant by the *terms of trade*?

9. What assumptions are made in introducing a second country into the life-cycle model? What do they imply about the real and nominal exchange rates?

10. Assuming constant and equal money demand parameters as well as factor price equalization, what determines the nominal exchange rate between two countries in the life-cycle model? What happens to the domestic exchange rate if the domestic money supply rises faster than that of the other country?

11. "The fiscal policy of a small open economy will be ineffective in altering either its capital-labor ratio, its real wage, or its real interest rate." Explain.

12. Why is it said that a country can control either its money supply or its exchange rate, but not both?

13. Under a flexible exchange rate system with no nominal rigidities, what are the real and nominal effects of a rise in the domestic money supply? What are the effects on the foreign price and the exchange rate?

14. In the context of foreign exchange, what is meant by *intervention*?

15. What are the arguments raised in support of and against fixed and flexible exchange rate systems?

16. How does the open economy IS curve differ from the derived in the closed economy model? Why? What are the implications for the effectiveness of fiscal and monetary policy in a small economy that faces nominal rigidities?

17. "With a fixed exchange rate, neither fiscal nor monetary policy will be able to raise a small open economy's output and employment." Explain.

Numerical Questions

1. Below are the price levels for three countries: A, B, and C.

Year	P_t^A	P_t^B	P_t^C
1996	100.0	100.0	100.0
1997	103.0	110.0	101.0
1998	106.1	121.0	116.2
1999	109.3	133.1	124.3

a. For country A, compute the nominal exchange rate over the years 1996 through 1999 consistent with purchasing power parity with each of the other two countries (e_t^{AB} and e_t^{AC}). Do the same for country B (e_t^{BA} and e_t^{BC}) and country C (e_t^{CA} and e_t^{CB}). Altogether, you will have computed six exchange rate series. Which pairs of the series are reciprocals?

b. Do country A's two exchange rates behave similarly over time? Explain the time path of each series. Do the same for countries B and C.

2. Below is a table containing information on consumer prices in the U.S. and Japan as well as the U.S. nominal exchange rate with Japan.

	Consumer Prices (1982-1984 = 100)		e_t (Yen/$)
Year	U.S.	Japan	
1987	113.6	104.9	144.60
1988	118.3	105.7	128.17
1989	124.0	108.0	138.07
1990	130.7	111.4	145.00
1991	136.2	115.0	134.59

a. For each year, compute for the U.S. the value of its real exchange rate with Japan. Do these figures demonstrate purchasing power parity?

b. Are these figures consistent with the statement made in the text regarding the short-run relationship between nominal and real exchange rates? Explain.

3. Below is a table containing money supply figures for Lower and Upper Slobovia. Their respective labor force sizes are 10 and 100.

	Money Supply	
Year	Lower Slobovia	Upper Slobovia
1996	200	1000
1997	300	1500
1998	375	1650
1999	375	1980

a. You live in Upper Slobovia. For each year, compute your country's nominal exchange rate with Lower Slobovia.

b. Explain the time path of the exchange rate series in terms of relative growth rates of the money supply.

Analytical Questions

1. For each of the following events, identify whether an appreciation, a depreciation, a revaluation, or a devaluation has occurred.

a. What has happened to the yen if the yen-dollar exchange rate changes from 105 to 120?

b.   What has happened to the deutsche mark if the German government changes the fixed franc-deutsche mark exchange rate from 3.5 to 3.8?

c.   What has happened to the U.S. Dollar if the U.S. government intervenes to push the Canadian dollar-U.S. dollar exchange rate from 1.3 to 1.4?

d.   What has happened to the dollar if the pound-dollar exchange rate changes from 0.5 to 0.7?

e.   What has happened to the lira if the Italian government changes the fixed lira-deutsche mark exchange rate from 980 to 1000?

2.   Suppose that there are two countries, Big and Bigger, that each produce a set of freely traded goods. The cost of the set of goods in Big is 150 bigbucks (150 bb), and the cost of the set of goods in Bigger is 100 biggerbucks (100 BB). The bigbuck per biggerbuck (bb/BB) exchange rate, which is set by the governments in a fixed exchange rate regime, currently is 1.5 bb/BB.

a.   Calculate the bigbuck per biggerbuck purchasing power parity exchange rate and compare it to the prevailing exchange rate. Is an exchange rate, realignment needed?

b.   Suppose that a technological innovation in Big causes the price of goods to fall to 125 bb. Recalculate the purchasing power parity exchange rate, and compare it to that found in part a. Explain any difference.

c.   Compare the prevailing exchange rate to the new purchasing power parity exchange rate. Is the bigbuck appropriately valued, overvalued, or undervalued?

d.   Suppose that you are a foreign currency trader. Given your assessment in part c, is the time right for a speculative attack on the bigbuck? If so, how would you proceed?

3.   Suppose that there are two countries, Ipso and Facto, that are identical in every way. Capital is completely mobile between the two countries, but labor is completely immobile. The currency unit in Ipso is the spam, and the currency unit in Facto is the velveeta. The money supply in each country is fixed, and money demand in each country is insensitive to changes in the interest rate. Suddenly, a technological improvement occurs in Ipso, but not in Facto.

a.   What happens to the capital-labor ratio in Ipso compared to that in Facto? Why?

b.   Assuming constant money supplies, what happens to the nominal spam per velveeta exchange rate? Why?

c.   Suppose that capital is immobile but labor is mobile when the technological change occurs. Are your conclusions about the effect on the nominal exchange rate the same as or different from those in part b? Why?

4.   The chapter ended with a discussion of the move to a single European currency. What are the implications of the new currency system for the individual countries' use of monetary and fiscal policies?

PART FIVE: ENRICHING THE MODEL

Chapter 14: The Banking System, the Federal Reserve, and the Money Supply

Chapter Outline

Introduction

Understanding financial intermediaries
    Financial intermediaries and our model
    Balance sheets of financial intermediaries
    Liabilities of financial intermediaries and U.S. monetary aggregates

Banks as special financial intermediaries
    Banks as repositories of money and issuers of liquid liabilities
    Bank reserves and the expansion of demand deposits

The money multiplier and the monetary base

The Federal Reserve and the conduct of monetary policy
    Structure and governance of the Federal Reserve System
    Mechanisms of monetary control
    Open market operations
    Using open market operations to finance government expenditures
    Lending through the discount window
    Reserve requirements

How well does the Fed control the money supply?
    Divergent paths of the monetary aggregates
    Understanding the variability of the monetary aggregates
    Case study: Monetary control during the Great Depression
    Should the Fed target the growth of monetary aggregates or interest rates?
    Case study: Paul Volcker's experiment in money supply targeting
    The endogeneity of the money supply

Bank runs and deposit insurance

Case study: The banking panic of the Great Depression and the establishment
of deposit insurance
Problems caused by deposit insurance and the need for bank regulation
Case study: The S&L crisis

Chapter summary

Key Terms

Bank reserves
Bank runs
Currency-deposit ratio (*cd*)
Deposit insurance
Discount rate
Discount window lending
Endogenous monetary policy
Excess reserves
Federal funds rate
Federal Reserve System
Financial intermediary
M1, M2, M3
M1 money multiplier
Monetary aggregates
Monetary base
Monetization
Moral hazard
Open market operation
Reserve-deposit ratio (*rd*)
Reserve requirements

Key Equations

M1 money multiplier:
$$\frac{M1}{MB} = \frac{cd + 1}{cd + rd}$$

QUESTIONS FOR CHAPTER 14

Review Questions

1.   What are *financial intermediaries*, and what functions do they perform? What special role do banks play? Provide some examples of other financial intermediaries.

2.   With regard to a financial institution's *balance sheet*, which assets are the most liquid? Which liabilities are the most liquid? Under what circumstances would *owners' equity* be negative?

3.   Define each of the following concepts and comment on any relationships among them.
       a.   *Demand deposits*
       b.   The *reserve-deposit ratio*
       c.   *Excess reserves*
       d.   Being *loaned up*
       e.   The M1 *money multiplier*, assuming all money is deposited in banks in the form of demand deposits and held as reserves (i.e., people hold no currency)

4.   What is the *monetary base*? How do the formula for and value of the M1 *money multiplier* change if people choose to hold some fraction of money in the form of currency? Explain intuitively (not just mathematically) why the formula changes.

5.   What are the privileges and responsibilities of banks associated with the *Federal Reserve System*? In what way does depositing reserves at the Fed constitute a cost to participating banks?

6.   Describe the institutional characteristics of the Fed's *Board of Governors* and the *Federal Open Market Committee*.

7.   What are the three principal tools used by the Fed to control the money supply? What would the Fed do with each of them if it wished to increase the money supply? if it wished to reduce the money supply?

8.   What does it mean for government borrowing to be *monetized*? What two agencies are involved? Do they work together to accomplish this task?

9. Why do banks borrow from the *discount window*? Where else do they borrow funds? What are the names of the interest rates paid in each of those markets? What would influence which market a bank would enter for funds? How does such borrowing affect the monetary base? Why?

10. The Fed can directly control the size of the monetary base but can only indirectly influence the size of the money multipliers. Comment, being sure to explain why the Fed has either direct or indirect control over the elements of the money supply.

11. Have the *monetary aggregates* behaved similarly over time? What implications does this behavior have for the conduct and measurement of monetary policy?

12. Explain the dramatic drop in M1 at the outset of the Great Depression. In particular, did the Fed explicitly engage in contractionary policy at that time? According to Friedman and Schwartz, what should the Fed have done at the time?

13. How are *nominal shocks* and *real shocks* characterized in the IS-LM model? Explain the effects of interest rate targeting and money supply targeting under each type of shock. What is the most appropriate target under each of the shocks? Why?

14. Explain the change in targeting (often referred to as a "regime change") that occurred under Fed Chairman Paul Volcker in the period from 1979 to 1982. What were the effects of the change? How accurate was the targeting itself?

15. What is meant by *endogenous monetary policy*? If the public expects a higher price level, what will happen if the Fed chooses not to print more money? What if it does print more money?

16. What is a *bank run*, and how does one typically start? What were the consequences of bank runs in the 1930s? What public policy changes have been made since then to improve the financial stability of banks and savings and loan institutions?

17. What is meant by the term *moral hazard*? Why is the concept important in banking?

Numerical Questions

1. Answer parts a through d using the following parameter values: $rd = 0.1$ and $cd = 0.4$.
   a. Calculate the value of the money multiplier.
   b. Suppose that rd rises to 0.2. Assuming the initial value for cd, calculate the new value of the money multiplier. Compare your answer to that obtained in part a. Provide economic intuition for any difference.
   c. Suppose that cd falls to 0.3. Assuming the initial value for rd, calculate the new value of the money multiplier. Compare your answer to that obtained in part a. Provide economic intuition for any difference.

2. Suppose that individuals hold their financial wealth totally as demand deposits and that banks hold as cash reserves 10 percent of any demand deposits. Suppose also that the Fed buys a $100 T-bill from a bank.
   a. Does the open market purchase itself, (i.e., prior to the issuance of bank loans) change the money supply? Why or why not?
   b. What are the values of the first three loans that are made in the money creation process? How much money is created by the first three loans?
   c. How does the monetary base change as a result of the open market purchase? Does the monetary base change further as loans are made?
   d. Suppose that individuals choose to hold as cash 20 percent of any amount loaned to them. How much money is created by the first three loans?

3. Answer parts a through c using the following parameter values: $rd = 0.05$, $cd = 0.3$, and the monetary base is $200.
   a. Calculate the values of the money multiplier and M1.
   b. Suppose that cd falls to 0.2. What is the new value of M1? If the Fed desires to change reserve requirements so as to return M1 to its initial value, at what value must it set rd?
   c. Suppose again that cd drops to 0.2. If the Fed desires to change the monetary base so as to return M1 to its initial value, at what value must it set the base?

Analytical Questions

1. Suppose that a bank uses its cash reserves to buy a T-bill from a private securities dealer instead of using the reserves to make loans. Will the impact on the money supply be different than if the bank makes a loan of equal value?

2.   Reserve requirements are a feature of many economies. Yet their use is often criticized. Some commentators argue that the requirements serve no useful purpose. Others claim that reserve requirements raise costs and put banks at a competitive disadvantage relative to other financial intermediaries.

   a.   Demonstrate that reserve requirements cannot by themselves guarantee that banks will have sufficient funds to meet depositor withdrawals. (In doing so, it might help to use balance sheet accounts.)

   b.   Explain how reserve requirements raise the costs to banks of acquiring funds from depositors for use in making loans.

3.   "Insurance companies and commercial banks perform exactly the same function. Only the details of the operations differ." Comment.

Chapter 15: Saving Behavior and Credit Markets

Chapter Outline

Introduction

Precautionary saving
        Impact of uncertainty on saving and capital formation: an example
        Private insurance and its impact on capital formation
        Government's provision of social insurance
        Types of government insurance
        How important is precautionary saving?

Saving and bequests
        Impact of bequests on capital accumulation
        Case study: Private intergenerational transfers and total U.S. wealth
        Life span uncertainty, annuities, and unintended bequests
        Case study: The increasing annuitization of the elderly in the United States
        Intentional bequests and gifts
        Intergenerational altruism and Ricardian equivalence
        Case study: Are U.S. extended families altruistically linked?

Modeling credit markets
        The demand for credit
        The supply of credit
        Capital accumulation in the presence of borrowing
        Credit market imperfections
        Why borrowing rates may exceed lending rates
        Case study: Credit liberalization and the decline in Norwegian saving
        Case study: Are U.S. citizens credit constrained?

Chapter summary

Key Terms

        Annuity
        Bequests
        Credit constraint
        Credit controls

Intervivos transfers
Precautionary saving
Ricardian equivalence
Risk aversion
Social insurance

Key Equations

Transition equation w/ bequests:
$$k_{t+1} = A(1-\beta)k_t^\beta - f_t - d_t$$

Transition equation w/ borrowing:
$$k_{t+1} = (1-m)w_t - m\frac{w_{t+1}}{1+r_{t+1}}$$

Key Graphs

Transition curve with bequests:

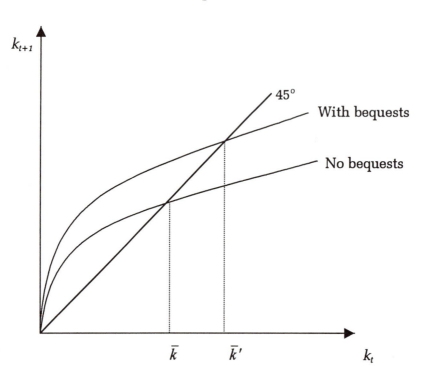

QUESTIONS FOR CHAPTER 15

Review Questions

1. What is *risk aversion*? What implications does it have for the amount of saving? What impact does risk aversion have on the transition diagram and the steady-state capital-labor ratio?

2. How can *insurance* affect the amount of *income uncertainty* that individuals face? What implications does the existence of insurance have for saving and the steady-state capital-labor ratio?

3. What factors can limit the provision of private insurance? How can the government's provision of insurance overcome some of the difficulties faced by private insurers? Give some examples of government insurance programs.

4. What effect do *bequests* have on the transition diagram and the steady-state capital-labor ratio?

5. What are *annuities*? How do annuities affect the amount of bequests that are made? What impact do annuities have on the transition diagram and the steady-state capital-labor ratio? What has happened during the past few decades to the fraction of the elderly's resources that is annuitized?

6. What are *intervivos transfers*? Give some examples. What implications do intervivos transfers have for government intergenerational transfer programs? How important are intervivos transfers in explaining individuals' consumption and saving behavior?

7. How are *borrowing* and *lending* incorporated into the life-cycle model? How is the *lifetime budget constraint* faced by borrowers written? What expression describes the total amount of credit demanded at a point in time? What expression describes the total amount of saving at a point in time? What impact does the existence of borrowing have on the transition diagram and the steady-state capital-labor ratio?

8. What does it mean to say an individual is *credit-constrained*? How can such a situation arise?

9. What are *lending rates*? What are *borrowing rates*? Why might the two differ in magnitude?

10. In the life-cycle model, what impact do *credit constraints* have on the transition diagram and the steady-state capital-labor ratio?

Numerical Questions

1. Consider an economy that is characterized by the following parameters: $A = 4$, $\alpha = 0.5$, and $\beta = 0.3$.
   a. What is the steady-state capital-labor ratio and level of individual income?
   b. Beginning with the steady state, assume that all individuals face uncertainty about second-period income. Specifically, individuals face a 50-50 chance of receiving or losing $1. Trace the value of the capital-labor ratio and the level of individual income for the next three periods, assuming individuals are risk-averse as described in the text.
   c. What effect does precautionary saving have on capital formation and income?

2. Suppose an economy's parameters are as follows: $A = 10$, $\alpha = 0.4$, and $\beta = 0.3$.
   a. What is the steady-state capital-labor ratio and level of individual income?
   b. Beginning with the steady state, assume that all individuals in all subsequent periods decide to bequeath 2 units of output to their offspring. Trace the value of the capital-labor ratio and the level of individual income for the next three periods. What effect do bequests have on capital formation and income?

Analytical Questions

1. Suppose that someone offers you two deals. In the first, you have a 50 percent chance of winning $4 and a 50 percent chance of winning nothing. In the second, you are certain to get $2.
   a. If you are risk-averse, which deal do you prefer?
   b. Assume that the second deal is modified so that you are only sure to receive $1. If you are risk-averse, which deal do you prefer in this case?

2. Suppose that you are in the business of lending money. Careful research has shown that you lose 2 percent of all the money that you lend, although different groups have different default rates. Specifically, you lose 2 percent of the money loaned to people with red hair, 1 percent of the money loaned to

people with black hair, and 3 percent of the money loaned to people with blond hair. Because everyone knows the default rates, people with red or blond hair dye their hair black so that they appear to be better risks. Finally, suppose that you loan equal amounts to people of different hair color, and that the risk-free lending rate is 10 percent.

a.   Assume that you are neither risk-averse nor a risk lover. If a person asks you for a loan, what is the minimum interest rate that you will charge? If you are risk-averse, how will your calculation differ?

b.   Suppose that the hair dye factory blows up, making it impossible for people to dye their hair. Once again, assuming that you are neither risk-averse nor a risk lover, what is the minimum interest rate that you will charge people of different hair color? How does risk aversion alter your calculation?

3.   Consider four individuals. John, who owns a tailor shop, and his friend Bob, who lives down the hall, work in the current period. They lend their current income and wait until next period to consume. Andy and Ben plan on writing a book and earning money from it next period. They wish to consume in this period but not in the next period. To consume now they must borrow from John and Bob and promise to repay the money with interest next period. Assume that Jon and Bob each earn $1,000 and that Andy and Ben expect to earn $550 each in the future. Also, assume that the interest rate next period, r_{t+1}, is 10 percent.

a.   How much will Andy and Ben each consume this period?

b.   How much saving will be devoted to capital formation in the current period?

c.   Suppose that unbeknownst to Andy and Ben, Jon and Bob receive inside information that a book like Andy and Ben's will be published next period and will likely reduce their earnings by half. Consequently, John and Bob will lend only half as much as before. How much are Ben and Andy able to consume in this case?

d.   Under the circumstances described in part c, how much saving will be devoted to capital formation? How does your answer compare to that in part b? Explain any difference.

4.   Assume the same initial situation described in question 3. Now suppose that the government levies a current-period tax on Andy and Ben of $100.

a.   What is the value of Andy and Ben's generational account?

b.   In what direction and by how much will Andy and Ben's consumption change as a result of the tax?

c.   Suppose that the government decides to levy a tax of $110 on Andy and Ben in the next period rather than $100 in the current period. What impacts does this fiscal policy change have on Andy and Ben's generational accounts and consumption? Explain.

d.   Suppose that Andy and Ben are credit-constrained, so that each consumes $200 less than his preferred amount. Under these circumstances, what effects would shifting the tax liability from $100 in the current period to $110 in the following period have on Andy and Ben's generational accounts and consumption? Explain.

5.   In the early 1980s, the Federal Reserve imposed limits on the amounts of consumer credit that lenders could provide. Analyze the likely short-run and long-run impacts of this policy on output. When discussing the possible short-run effects, discuss alternative outcomes that could arise depending on whether nominal price rigidity is present.

Chapter 16: Financial Markets and the Investment Decision

Chapter Outline

Introduction

Anatomy of postwar U.S. investment

The incentive to invest
    User cost of capital
        Accounting for depreciation
        The user cost: a numerical example

Corporate income tax, user cost of capital, and investment
    Corporate income tax
    Relating changes in the user cost to changes in investment
    Effects of sector-specific taxation

Tax policy and capital's user cost in practice
    Case study: Housing investment in the 1980s
    A note on expectations

Corporate financial policy
    Debt-equity decision
    Debt and taxes
    Case study: Interest rate spreads and the business cycle
    Case study: Corporate borrowing in the 1980s
    Case study: Credit constraints in the United States and Japan

Understanding investment dynamics
    Irreversibility
    Case study: The empty office buildings
    Adjustment lags
    Case study: Investment and the stock market: Tobin's q-theory

Chapter summary

Key Terms

Accelerated depreciation
Adjustment lag
Capital accumulation
Capital structure of a firm
Corporate income tax
Efficient markets hypothesis
Internal finance
Investment incentives
Investment tax credit
Irreversibility
Modigliani-Miller Theorem
Tobin's q-theory
User cost of capital
Yield spread

Key Equations

User cost of capital w/ depreciation and corporate taxes:

$$MPK = r + \delta + \tau$$

QUESTIONS FOR CHAPTER 16

Review Questions

1. What is *investment spending*? On average, how much U.S. GDP is devoted to investment goods?

2. What is *fixed investment*, and what subcategories of investment goods does it include? What is *inventory investment*, and what are some examples of inventory investment?

3. Describe how the *composition* of fixed investment spending has changed over the past three decades. Identify some possible reasons for these trends.

4. What is the *user cost of capital*? What factors does the basic (before tax) user cost of capital include? What is the equation for the basic user cost of capital?

How does knowledge of the user cost help a firm decide how much capital investment it should undertake?

5. What is the tax base for the *corporate income tax*? How does the existence of the corporate income tax affect the user cost of capital?

6. What does the *demand schedule for capital* indicate, and how is it derived? What slope does the demand schedule have (positive or negative), and why? How does an increase in the rate of depreciation affect the demand schedule? How is the demand schedule affected by an increase in the tax per dollar of capital?

7. Identify three reasons why the *supply* of capital might depend on the real interest rate.

8. What are government *investment incentives*, and what is their purpose? Give examples of two important investment incentives. What effect do investment incentives have on the cost of capital? Why does it make sense for the government to levy a tax on corporate income and simultaneously offer investment incentives?

9. Describe the possibly different effects that *permanent* versus *temporary* tax changes might have. What problems might arise from the use of a temporary tax change?

10. What is a firm's *financial policy*? Define the terms *securities, bonds, debt* and *equity* as they relate to a firm's financial policy.

11. What is the *Modigliani-Miller theorem*? What practicalities does the Modigliani-Miller theorem ignore?

12. What is the *yield spread*, and what does it indicate?

13. What types of firms are *credit-constrained* in the United States? What is a Japanese *keiretsu*? How do keiretsus diminish the extent of credit rationing in Japan?

14. What is meant by the *irreversibility* of investment? What types of capital are most subject to irreversibility?

15. What are *adjustment lags*, and why do they arise?

16.   What is *Tobin's q*? What does Tobin's *q*-theory impact about investment spending? Is there empirical support for the theory?

Numerical Questions

1.   Suppose that a firm owns two types of capital, half of which is durable equipment and half of which is nonresidential structures. The annual depreciation rate for equipment is 20 percent and that for structures is 4 percent. Also, assume that the real interest rate equals 12 percent and that the tax component of the user cost of capital (τ) equals 5 percent.
   a.   Compute the basic, before-tax, user cost of capital for equipment and for structures.
   b.   Compute the average user cost of capital.
   c.   Compute the full, tax-inclusive, user cost of capital for each type of capital and for the capital stock as a whole.
   d.   Suppose that Congress enacts a 2 percent investment tax credit for producers' durable equipment. Compute the new user cost of capital for equipment and for structures.
   e.   Compute the new average user cost of capital (including the effect of the tax credit), assuming that, at the margin, the proportions of each type of capital purchased remain unchanged.

2.   Assume the economy is characterized as in the life-cycle model of Chapter 3 (i.e., no fiscal policy term, no international trade, and no money or price level). Specifically, assume that the economy's parameter values are $A = 10$, $\alpha = 0.3$, and $\beta = 0.4$.
   a.   There is presently no tax on capital and capital does not depreciate. For values of the real interest rate, r, from 0.1 to 0.9 by increments of 0.1, compute the values of the user cost of capital and the demand for capital.
   b.   Suppose that a capital tax τ of 2 percent is imposed and that capital depreciates at a rate of 10 percent. For values of the real interest rate, r, from 0.1 to 0.9 by increments of 0.1, compute the values of the user cost of capital and the demand for capital.
   c.   Explain what has happened to the position of the demand curve for capital because of the introduction of the corporate income tax and depreciation.

3.   Using the same parameter values as in question 2 ($A = 10$, $\alpha = 0.3$, and

$\beta = 0.4$), compute the equilibrium values of the capital-labor ratio, k, and the real interest rate, r, under the following conditions.

    a.   There is no tax on capital and no depreciation.

    b.   The tax on capital is 2 percent, and the depreciation rate is 10 percent. Is your result consistent with the shift in the demand curve for capital obtained in question 2 above? Explain.

4.   Suppose that the saving propensity is now directly related to the interest rate— that is, the consumption propensity α is inversely related to the interest rate. Specifically, assume that the formula for the consumption propensity is $\alpha = 0.5 - 0.14r$.

    a.   For values of the real interest rate, r, from 0.1 to 0.9 by increments of 0.1, compute the values of the supply of capital. (Helpful hint: Solve the steady-state capital-labor ratio equation replacing α with the formula given above.)

    b.   What relationship is there between the real interest rate and the quantity of capital supplied? What is the intuition behind this relationship?

5.   a.   Using the demand relationships developed in questions 2 and 3 and the supply relationship developed in question 4, verify that the equilibrium when there is no corporate income tax and no depreciation happens to be the same as in question 3. That is, verify that the equilibrium interest rate and capital-labor ratio are as before. (Helpful hint: Substitute the old equilibrium interest rate into both the demand schedule and the supply schedule, and verify that the values of k in the two schedules are equal.)

    b.   Solve for the new equilibrium interest rate upon introduction of the tax on capital and depreciation. What is the equilibrium value of the capital-labor ratio? (See the hint in part a.)

    c.   How do your results in part b differ from those obtained in question 3b? That is, when the saving propensity is directly related to the interest rate rather than being constant, what effect do changes in taxes or depreciation rates have on the resulting values of r and k? Explain the intuition.

Analytical Questions

1.   The chapter discussed the use of the investment tax credit as an investment incentive. Critics of the investment tax credit argue that it is an inefficient

incentive, in that the government ends up forgoing a lot of tax revenue per dollar of additional investment undertaken.

    a.   What aspect(s) of the investment tax credit might result in the shortcoming identified by the critics?

    b.   An alternative investment tax credit has been proposed, which applies only to a firm's investment spending that exceeds a specified percentage of past years' investment spending. Would this variant of the credit be a more efficient investment incentive?

    c.   What are some practical shortcomings of the alternative tax credit scheme described in part b?

2.   Suppose that a firm can raise funds for investment either by issuing bonds (debt) or by issuing shares of stock (equity). The market interest rate on bonds is r, and the rate on stock is e. The firm faces a depreciation rate of δ per dollar of capital and a tax liability of τ per dollar of capital.

    a.   Assuming that a firm raises funds only by issuing equity, write the expression describing the firm's user cost of capital.

    b.   Now assume that the firm raises 40 percent of its funds by issuing debt and 60 percent by issuing equity. Write the expression describing the firm's user cost of capital.

    c.   Finally, assuming that the firm raises funds as in part b, suppose that Congress allows firms to deduct the interest payment on debt for purposes of computing taxable income. Write the expression describing the firm's user cost of capital. Assume that the corporate income tax is equal to c.

ANSWERS TO EVEN-NUMBERED QUESTIONS

Chapter 1: Output, Inputs, and Growth

Review Questions

2.   A stock variable measures an amount *at a specific time.* A flow variable is a
        value given *over an interval of time.* Classic examples of the two are *wealth*
        (stock) and *income* (flow). A stock variable is often the result of the flow over
        time. Flow variables generally have some time measure associated with them
        (e.g. *hourly wage*).

size of the labor force	stock
investment	flow
depreciation	flow
real GDP	flow
an office building	stock
current state of technology	stock

4.   Labor and capital are the key inputs to production. *Labor* includes all of the
        human inputs (including the effort supplied by workers, managers, and owners
        of business enterprises). Labor is typically measured by the number of hours
        worked.
        Capital includes all of the *non-human* inputs (including buildings, inventories,
        residential structures, and consumer durables). Capital is measured in terms of
        its price in real (or constant) dollars so that the measure is not inflated by a
        change in its market price.

6.   *Multifactor productivity* measures how well we turn inputs into output. We
        often think of it as a measure of *technology* or *efficiency*. In the Cobb-Douglas
        production function, we describe multifactor productivity with the variable A.
        Since technology is very hard to measure, we calculate a value for A by
        substituting values of output (Y), capital (K), and labor (L) into the function, and
        then solving for A.
        Embodied productivity changes take place when there are changes in the
        quality of the input. For example, better-educated workers tend to be a more
        productive input into the production process.
        Disembodied productivity changes take place when there is a change in the
        process of production. For example, the introduction of the assembly line led
        to greater output in automobile production.

8. *Labor productivity* (y) is a measure of output per unit of labor input (often stated as "output per worker"). It is measured as total output divided by total labor:

$$y = Y/L$$

The *marginal product of labor*, however, is the additional output produced with one additional unit of labor, holding the amount of capital fixed (defined in chapter 3).
Since the Cobb-Douglas production function exhibits diminishing marginal returns, an increase in labor will *decrease* the marginal product of labor. An increase in capital, however, provides a larger amount of capital for the marginal worker, so it will *increase* the marginal product of labor.

10. The *standard of living* is measured as *GDP per capita* or output per person. The standard of living has roughly quadrupled since 1929. More recently, GDP per capita was $20,964 in 1970, for total growth of about 25 percent by 1996, or average annual growth of less than one percent over that time period. Other developed countries have also seen lower growth rates in recent years. Some developing countries have been growing more rapidly than the more developed countries, while others have experienced very low rates of growth.

Numerical Questions

2.   a.   What is the total amount of capital owned by the company?
2 copiers:	2($1000)	= $2000
8 personal computers:	8($800)	= $6400
Total capital:		= $8400

b.   Copiers depreciate by 20% per year, while personal computers depreciate by 40% per year. Thus, in two years the capital stock will be worth:
2 copiers:	(.8)(.8)($2000)	= $1280
8 personal computers:	(.6)(.6)($6400)	= $2304
Total capital:		= $3584

c.   If the company buys an additional computer after year 1 for $800, then after two years, the capital stock of the company will equal:
Total from part (b):		= $3584
additional computer (.6)($800)		= $480
Total capital:		= $4064

4. Using the Cobb-Douglas production function with $K = 200$, $L = 100$, $A = 2$, $\beta = 0.4$.

   a. intensive form production:
   $$y = A k^{\beta}$$
   $$y = (2)(200/100)^{0.4} = 2.64$$

   b. with $k = 4$:
   $$y = (2)(4)^{0.4} = 3.48$$

   c. The answer to (b) does not depend on why the value of k changed since y is a function of k itself.

   d. Suppose $A = 3$, with $k = 2$: $y = (3)(2)^{0.4} = 3.96$
   The 50% increase in A resulted in a 50% increase in y.

Analytical Questions

2. The growth accounting model uses the formula:

   $$\Delta Y/Y = \Delta A/A + \beta \, \Delta K/K + (1-\beta) \, \Delta L/L$$

   That is, there are three possible sources of growth in output: changes in technology, increases in the capital stock, and changes in the labor force. Of the three, increases in multifactor productivity will lead to a one-for-one increase in output, while changes in capital and labor will lead to smaller output changes. In a free-market system, resources tend to flow to their highest *value* in the market. Since technology changes give the greatest change in output, it is profitable to pursue more efficient methods of production. Under centralized economic planning, the rewards of the market are not available to innovators, so there is not likely to be as much innovation.

Chapter 2: The Dynamic Supply of Inputs

Review Questions

2. *Direct owners* of physical capital have control or possession of the capital. *Indirect owners* of physical capital have a legal claim to the income generated by the capital. About half of the U.S. stock of *physical capital* is owned *directly* by U.S. households. The rest of the stock is directly owned by businesses. Since households ultimately own the businesses, the households are *indirect* owners of that part of the capital stock.

4. Given a specific amount of income, the consumption and saving decisions are made at the same time. One way to define saving is as "the amount of income that was not consumed." But the amount that is saved allows consumption to be deferred to a later time by allowing the person to accumulate assets. Thus saving could also be defined as "the amount of assets held."

6.
consumption:	c_{yt} c_{ot+1}
wage:	w_t
interest rate:	r_{t+1}
number of young people:	N
number of old people:	N

   young person's saving $= w_t - c_{yt}$
   old person's assets $= a_{t+1} = w_t - c_{yt}$
   total labor force $= N$
   total capital stock $= N\, a_{t+1}$
   old person's consumption $= c_{ot+1} = a_{t+1}\,(1 + r_{t+1})$

8. *Lifetime budget constraint:* $c_{yt} + c_{ot+1}/(1+r_{t+1}) = w_t$

   The individual has no control over the wage rate or the interest rate, but he or she may choose any feasible combination of consumption when young and consumption when old. To be feasible, the left-hand side of the budget constraint must be less than or equal to the right-hand side (the wage). If the left-hand side is less than the wage, then the person is not consuming the maximum amount (part of the wage is being wasted).
   The lifetime budget constraint is graphed with c_{ot+1} on the vertical axis and c_{yt} on the horizontal axis. The horizontal intercept (maximum consumption when young if consumption when old is zero) is equal to w_t. The vertical intercept (maximum consumption when old, if consumption when young is zero) is

$w_t (1 + r_{t+1})$. Thus the slope of the lifetime budget constraint is $-(1+r_{t+1})$.

Lifetime budget constraint:

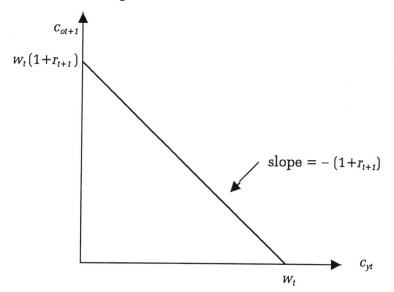

10.   The *utility function* measures the amount of utility (or happiness or well-being) that an individual receives from consuming the amounts c_{yt} and c_{ot+1}, which is dependent on the preference parameter α. The Cobb-Douglas utility function is written: $u_t = c_{yt}^{\alpha} c_{ot+1}^{1-\alpha}$

Time preference is indicated by the size of the parameter α. A relatively large value for α indicates that individuals have a strong preference (or desire) for consumption when they are young. A relatively small value for α indicates that individuals have a stronger preference for consumption when they are old.

12.   In the life-cycle model, all saving by the young is held as assets, which are then used as the capital stock. At the same time, however, the old are *dissaving*, or converting all of their assets into consumption, since they have no income from wages when they are retired. Thus, *national saving* is equal to the difference between the saving of the young and the dissaving of the old. Since the assets are used as capital, the change in the capital stock must equal the difference in the amount of assets held, that is,

$N a_{t+1} - N a_t$ must equal $K_{t+1} - K_t$

We can also look at national saving as the difference between total output and total consumption:
$$S_t = Y_t - N\,c_{yt} - N\,c_{ot}$$

By substituting $Y_t = N\,w_t + r_t\,K_t$, and rearranging, we get:
$$S_t = N\,(w_t - c_{yt}) + (r_t\,K_t - N\,c_{ot})$$

We know that $a_{t+1} = w_t - c_{yt}$, $K_t = a_t$, and that $c_{ot} = a_t\,(1 + r_t)$. Substituting and rearranging, we get:
$$S_t = N\,a_{t+1} - N\,a_t = K_{t+1} - K_t = I_t$$

14.   The age distribution of the U.S. population is expected to get older in coming decades as a result of the post-World War II baby boom. The U.S. population is projected to continue growing, but at a very low rate. As the population ages, the capital labor ratio may rise, since there will be more older people (who supply capital) and fewer young people (who supply labor) in the economy.

Numerical Questions

2.   Cobb-Douglas production function: $A = 4$, $K_0 = 300$, $N = 200$, $\alpha = 0.5$, $\beta = 0.3$

   a.   Output in period 0: $Y_0 = A\,K^{\beta}\,L^{(1-\beta)} = (4)(300)^{0.3}(200)^{0.7} = 903.48$

   b.   Income paid to labor: $w_0\,L_0 = (1 - \beta)\,Y_0 = (0.7)(903.48) = 632.44$

   c.   Income paid to a worker: $w_0 = (1 - \beta)\,Y_0 / L_0 = 632.44/200 = 3.16$

   d.   Income earned by capital: $r_0\,K_0 = \beta\,Y_0 = (0.3)(903.48) = 271.04$

   e.   interest rate: $r_0 = \beta\,Y_0 / K_0 = 271.04/300 = 0.90$

   f.   consumption and saving by the young:
$$c_{yo} = \alpha\,w_0 = (0.5)(3.16) = 1.58$$
$$a_1 = (1 - \alpha)\,w_0 = (0.5)(3.16) = 1.58$$

4.   a. $c_{01} = a_1\,(1 + r_1) = (1.58)(1.87) = 2.95$

   b. $u_0 = c_{yo}{}^{\alpha}\,c_{o1}{}^{1-\alpha} = (1.58)^{0.5}\,(2.95)^{0.5} = 2.16$

Analytical Questions

2.   If people place greater weight on future consumption than they did in the past, the lifecycle model would show a smaller value for the time preference parameter α. An decrease in α would lead people to save more of their wages (yielding a higher level of investment), leading to a higher future capital stock. Since the economy will have more capital to work with in the future, output will also be higher than it would have been otherwise.

4.   If the *MRS* is equal to –1.05 it means that the slope of the indifference curve at that consumption point is equal to –1.05. If the interest rate is equal to 10 percent, then the slope of the budget line is equal to –1.10. Therefore, the indifference curve *cannot* be tangent to the budget line at that combination of consumption when young and consumption when old. By saving one *more* unit of consumption, the individual would receive 1.1 unit more of consumption when old (more than the tradeoff shown by the *MRS*). Thus, the individual should decrease consumption when young and increase consumption when old until the *MRS* is equal to the slope of the budget line.

Chapter 3: The Dynamic Demand for Inputs and the Evolution of Output

Review Questions

2.   In the life-cycle model, it does not matter if the elderly lend their savings (buy corporate bonds) to firms instead of purchasing ownership in the firms (buy stock). *In either case, the elderly will receive the same return: the value of the capital itself, plus the return on that capital.* If the elderly lend their savings, then their return is paid as principal and interest on the bond. If the elderly buy stock, then their return is obtained from the price received by selling the stock plus any dividends paid by the firm.

4.   In the real world, the human capital of workers increases as they are trained and acquire more experience in their jobs. In our life-cycle model, however, we will simply assume that all workers are identical in skills, experience, talents, and education, and further, we assume that they don't gain any new skills on the job. In the model, workers only work for one period (while they are young), so there is no easy way to describe improvements in their human capital. In the real world, workers are employed for many periods (years), and often in many different jobs during their working lives. There are very few jobs in the real world where human capital is unimportant.

6.   *Input markets are competitive* when the individual suppliers of each input (capital or labor) are all *price takers.* That is, the individual workers cannot demand higher wages than the equilibrium wage (nor would they accept a lower wage), and the individual suppliers of capital cannot demand a higher interest rate than the equilibrium interest rate. In addition, there must be many firms in the market so that the buyers of inputs (the firms) are also price takers who must accept the equilibrium wage and interest rate as well.

8.   If more capital is used in production, the marginal product of capital (*MPK*) will *fall.* The $MPK = \beta Y / K$. To get the intensive-form equation for the *MPK*, first substitute the Cobb-Douglas production function for the value of Y and rearrange:

$$MPK = \beta A \, (K/L)^{\beta - 1}$$

If we substitute k for K/L, we get:

$$MPK = \beta A \, k^{\beta - 1}$$

If we increase the quantity of capital (K) holding labor constant, the value of the capital-labor ratio ($k = K/L$) will increase. Since the exponent $\beta-1$ is negative, the value of the MPK will fall, which is an example of *diminishing returns*.

Now consider the marginal product of labor (MPL):

$$MPL = (1 - \beta)\, Y/L = (1 - \beta)\, A\, (K/L)^{\beta} = (1 - \beta)\, A\, k^{\beta}$$

In this case, an increase in L will decrease the value of k, leading to a decrease in the MPL and *diminishing returns*. If on the other hand, we increase the amount of capital, the value of k increases, leading to a higher value for the MPL since the workers now have more capital to use in production.

10. When there are no changes in technology or the size of the labor force, the economy in the life-cycle model will eventually reach a *steady state*. In this steady state all of the variables in the model (output, consumption, capital per worker, the wage, the interest rate) are constant. If the economy is originally at a capital-labor ratio below the steady-state value, the economy will grow only until it reaches the steady state. As the capital-labor ratio grows, diminishing returns will mean that the benefit from the additional capital will be smaller and smaller.

12. *Endogenous growth models* particularly emphasize the role of technological change in economic growth by incorporating into the model decisions on research and development, education spending, and other actions that affect the state of technology. The life-cycle model introduced in the text assumes that all technological change is *exogenous* (or outside) the economic model. The life-cycle model could be expanded to include endogenous growth.

Numerical Questions

2.   a. and b.

Period	k_t	K_t	Y_t	w_t	r_t
0	1.5000	300.0000	903.4775	3.1622	0.9035
1	1.5811	316.2171	917.8604	3.2125	0.8708
2	1.6063	321.2511	922.2197	3.2278	0.8612
3	1.6139	322.7769	923.5315	3.2324	0.8584
4	1.6162	323.2360	925.9254	3.2337	0.8575
steady state	1.6172	323.4330	924.0943	3.2343	0.8571

c.   Total transition of the capital stock from period 0 to steady state

$$= \overline{K} - K_0 = 323.4330 - 300 = 23.4330$$

ΔK between period 0 and period 1 $= K_1 - K_0 = 316.2171 - 300 = 16.2171$

Percent of transition between periods 0 and 1 $= \dfrac{K_1 - K_0}{\overline{K} - K_0}$

$$= \frac{16.2171}{23.4330} = 0.6921$$

$$= 69.21\%$$

Percent of transition between periods 3 and 4 $= \dfrac{K_4 - K_3}{\overline{K} - K_0}$

$$= \frac{0.4591}{23.4330} = 0.0196$$

$$= 1.96\%$$

Growth of the capital stock slows as the economy approaches the steady state due to diminishing returns to capital.

d. All of the variables will be constant in the steady state. As the economy grows and the capital stock approaches the steady state level, the capital stock changes by smaller and smaller increments (see part c above). Eventually the change goes to zero. When the capital stock stops growing, the capital-labor ratio (k) will also be constant, as will output (Y). With output constant, saving and investment cannot change. With the capital-labor ratio constant, the wage rate and the interest rate cannot change.

4. a. and b. Assume that Period 0 is the steady state prior to the earthquake. One-third of the capital stock is destroyed between Period 0 and Period 1:

Period	k_t	K_t	Y_t	w_t	r_t
0	1.6172	323.4330	924.0943	3.2343	0.8571
1	1.0781	215.6220	818.2555	2.8639	1.1385
2	1.4319	286.3894	890.9802	3.1184	0.9333
3	1.5592	311.8431	914.0329	3.1991	0.8793
4	1.5996	319.9115	921.0643	3.2237	0.8637
5	1.6119	322.3725	923.1842	3.2311	0.8591
steady state	1.6172	323.4330	924.0943	3.2343	0.8571

c. The new steady-state values are identical to the old ones. Since there are no changes in α, β, or A, there is no change in the transition equation. Thus, since the steady-state capital-labor ratio is unchanged, the other steady-state variables are unchanged as well.

6. a. Assume $\beta = 0.25$:

	k_t	K_t	Y_t	w_t	r_t
steady state	1.7171	343.4143	915.7752	3.4342	0.6667

b. The most important difference between the two steady states is that the capital-labor ratio is higher when $\beta = 0.25$. With more capital per worker, there will be a larger capital stock. Output, however, will be lower since capital is now less productive. Since capital is relatively more abundant, the interest rate is lower and the wage rate is higher.

Analytical Questions

2. Profit $= Y - rK - wL$
   $MPK = \beta Y / K$
   $MPL = (1 - \beta) Y/L$
   Substituting $MPK = r$, and $MPL = w$:
   Profit $= Y - (\beta Y / K) K - ((1 - \beta) Y/L) L = Y - \beta Y - (1 - \beta) Y = 0$

4. "A country's standard of living can continue to rise only if there is ongoing technological change."
   In the standard life-cycle model, we assume that technology and population are constant. With those assumptions, the economy will converge to a steady state where all variables are constant. If we allowed population to grow at a constant rate, the size of the economy would grow (even in the steady state), but all of the per capita variables (k, y, w, and r) would be constant in the steady state. If technology grows at a constant rate, however, the aggregate and per capita variables in the model (k, K, y, Y, w, and r) would continue growing in the steady state. Thus, output per person would continue to rise indefinitely.

Chapter 4: Economic Fluctuations

Review Questions

2.   In recent decades, U.S. expansions have been about five times as long as recessions (five years vs. 11 months). If we look at data over the long period from 1854 to the present, it is clear that expansions have become longer and recessions have become shorter.

4.   A *broad-based, short-term cyclical fluctuation* is another term for a recession. A *long-term sectoral decline* describes a change within a particular industry or area of the economy (for example, the decline in U.S. textile production in the twentieth century). Macroeconomists distinguish between these two phenomena because they have different causes. The long-term sectoral declines are usually associated with changing tastes (a change in demand) and/or changing production costs (a change in supply). The broad-based, short-term fluctuations usually result from shocks to the economy (e.g. war, drought, an oil price shock) or macroeconomic instability (e.g. poor monetary policy).

6.   A person is *employed* if they currently hold a job.
A person is *unemployed* if they do not hold a job, but they are actively seeking work.
The *labor force* of an economy includes all adult individuals who are either employed or unemployed (as defined above).
Discouraged workers are individuals who were unemployed, but who stopped looking for work, and thus dropped out of the labor force. Discouraged workers are *not* counted as unemployed.
The *labor force participation rate* is calculated as the fraction of the adult population that is either employed or unemployed.

8.   *Capital utilization* is measured by the Federal Reserve System (the Fed). The measurement is an estimate of how much an industry is currently producing compared to its maximum *capacity* to produce. Maximum productive capacity is estimated by considering past output levels. Capital utilization is a procyclical variable.

10.   *Seasonal data adjustment* is an attempt to isolate and remove seasonal movements from economic time series. For example, agricultural production is not steady over the calendar year, because the growing season is a *seasonal cycle*. Obviously, economists should care more about the differences in

agricultural output from year to year than they care about the differences in agricultural output from April to May. By removing seasonal fluctuations from the data, economists are able to see business cycles more clearly, and are less likely to try to control things that are outside the realm of policy (e.g. seasonal agricultural output, seasonal holiday shopping, etc.).

12.   The *accelerator* is the relationship between the change in output from one year to the next and the amount of investment. In the life-cycle model, the equation for investment per worker is:

$$i_t = (1 - \alpha)(1 - \beta)(y_t - y_{t-1})$$

Thus, investment will change by the fraction $[(1 - \alpha)(1 - \beta)]$ of the change in output. This fraction is defined as the accelerator.

Numerical Questions

2.   Assuming $A = 4$, $N = 200$, $\alpha = 0.5$, and $\beta = 0.3$:

a.   Trace out the time path for the capital-labor ratio and output:

period	A	k	Y
0	4.0	1.6172	924.09
1	4.5	1.6172	1039.61
2	4.0	1.8193	957.33
3	4.0	1.6753	933.94
4	4.0	1.6344	927.04
5	4.0	1.6223	924.98

b. $\bar{k} = [(1-\alpha)(1-\beta)A]^{\frac{1}{1-\beta}} = [(0.5)(0.3)4]^{\frac{1}{0.7}} = 1.6172$

$\bar{Y} = A\bar{k}^{\beta}N = (4)(1.6172)^{0.3}(200) = 924.09$

The steady-state values did not change since α, β, and A are the same as before.

c.   In part a, output appears to illustrate an expansion in a business cycle. The technology shock increased productivity temporarily, as is illustrated in the real business cycle theory. Unlike a normal business cycle, however, the periods in our model last for a generation, so the cycle illustrated is much longer than the typical real-world business cycle. Part a also differs from a normal business cycle in that all resources are fully used at all times—there is no unemployment of capital or labor in this version of the life-cycle model.

Analytical Questions

2. The text states that according to real business cycle theory, "business cycles are caused by shocks to technology and household preferences and are therefore simply part of the economy's equilibrium path." By equilibrium path, we mean the movement of the economy from one steady state to the next. In some cases (such as numerical problem 2, above), the shock temporarily pushes the economy away from its steady state, and the equilibrium path moves it back to the same point. In other cases (such as a shock to household preferences that changes the value of α), the economy will converge to a new steady state. Since the economy is on an *equilibrium path*, we are still assuming that *all markets are in equilibrium*, so there are no unemployed resources. Thus a real business cycle theorist would *not* suggest that the government intervene in the economy. Any intervention would move the economy *away from equilibrium*.

Chapter 5: The Measurement of Output and Prices

Review Questions

2. *Final goods* are those that have been sold to their ultimate users, that is, they will not be sold again. *Intermediate goods* are those that will be used in the production of other goods, or those that will be resold by a business. For example, if a wool producer sells woolen yarn to a sweater manufacturer, then the wool is considered to be an intermediate good in the production of a sweater (final good). If on the other hand, the wool is sold directly to a consumer, then the wool itself is a final good. In fact, the wool is counted as a final good in this case, *even if* the consumer uses it to knit a sweater, since household production of goods is not counted in GDP.

   If all sales by businesses were counted in GDP, the figure would seriously overstate what is actually produced. Continuing with the example above, if we count the value of the wool *and* the value of the sweater, we would be double counting. Certainly the value of the sweater would already include the value of the inputs used in making it.

   The *value added method* of computing GDP considers the additional value created at each step of a production process. Value added is calculated as the difference between the cost of the inputs and the value of the thing that is sold.

4. *Gross domestic product (GDP)* is the market value of all final goods and services produced within a country in a given year.

   Net domestic product (NDP) is GDP adjusted for depreciation of the capital stock.

   National Income (NI) is equal to GNP (GDP plus net receipt of foreign factor income) less the sum of depreciation and indirect business taxes

   Personal Income (PI) equals before-tax income received by households, which is equal to national income minus retained earnings plus transfer payments.

   Disposable Income (DI) is equal to after-tax income received by households. It is calculated as personal income minus individual income taxes.

6. The *expenditure approach* to calculating GDP considers all of the uses of domestic output. Output can be used for *consumption* (C), *investment* (I), *government spending* (G), or it may be *exported*. *Imports* (M) must also be considered, however, since they will account for part of C, I, and G, but must not be counted as part of GDP. Thus, we know that GDP + M = C + I + G + X, or GDP = C + I + G + X − M.

Expenditures by individuals are primarily broken down into the types of consumption expenditures: durable goods, nondurable goods, and services. New private housing construction shows up as part of investment.

8.   A *quantity index* is used to measure changing quantities over time, holding prices constant. A *price index*, on the other hand, holds quantities fixed (for the CPI the quantities are in a fixed market basket) in order to measure changing prices. *Real GDP* in a given year is a measure of that year's output valued at some other year's prices, so it is a specific quantity index. Real GDP is now calculated using a chain weighting process to reduce the biases of using a particular base year. *Nominal GDP* is just the value of a given year's output valued at that year's prevailing prices.

10. A *price index* holds output quantities fixed (in the CPI the quantities are those in a fixed market basket) in order to measure changing prices. A *Laspeyres index* fixes quantities in a prior year, while a *Paasche index* fixes quantities in the current year. For example the CPI is a Laspeyres index since it calculates the current cost of some quantities purchased in the past. The GDP deflator, on the other hand, is a Paasche index since it calculates the value of current production using prices from the past.

12. The *Fisher Equation* is an estimate that states that the nominal interest rate is approximately equal to the real interest rate plus the inflation rate, or

$$i_{t+1} = r_{t+1} + \pi_{t+1}$$

The Fisher equation stipulates that individuals will negotiate a nominal interest rate on a loan by considering their *desired real interest rate* and *the expected (or anticipated) level of inflation*. The actual real interest rate that prevails, however, depends on the actual level of inflation over the life of the loan. The nominal interest rate and the inflation rate are easily observed (or reported in the news), allowing us to calculate the actual real interest rate after the fact.

Numerical Questions

2.   a.   GDP deflator = (Nominal GDP / Real GDP) × 100
         Nominal GDP_1= GDP deflator × Real GDP / 100
                     = (100)(300)/(100)
                     = 300

Note: in the base year, Nominal GDP = Real GDP

b. $\quad$ GDP deflator$_2$ = (900) / (600) × 100
$\qquad\qquad\qquad$ = 150

c. $\quad$ Real GDP$_3$ $\quad$ = (1500) / (300) × 100
$\qquad\qquad\qquad$ = 500

$\qquad$ Real GDP$_4$ $\quad$ = (1200) / (200) × 100
$\qquad\qquad\qquad$ = 600

d. $\quad$ There was a recession in period 3 since real GDP dropped from 600 in period 2 to 500 in period 3. By period 4, output had recovered to its previous level.

e. $\quad$ Deflation occurred in period 4 since the GDP deflator (a price index) dropped from 300 in period 3 to 200 in period 4.

4. $\quad$ a. $\quad$ Nominal GDP $\quad$ = $(P_f Q_f) + (P_c Q_c)$

$\qquad$ Nominal GDP$_{98}$ $\quad$ = (30 × 10) + (20 × 5) = 400

$\qquad$ Nominal GDP$_{99}$ $\quad$ = (45 × 20) + (25 × 7) = 1075

b. $\quad$ Real GDP (1998 base) $\quad$ = $(P_{f98} Q_f) + (P_{c98} Q_c)$

$\qquad$ Real GDP$_{98}$ $\qquad\qquad$ = (30 × 10) + (20 × 5) = 400

$\qquad$ Real GDP$_{99}$ $\qquad\qquad$ = (30 × 20) + (20 × 7) = 740

$\qquad$ Percentage change $\qquad$ = (740 − 400)/400 = 85%

c. $\quad$ GDP deflator $\qquad\quad$ = (Nominal GDP / Real GDP) × 100

$\qquad$ GDP deflator$_{98}$ $\qquad$ = (400) / (400) × 100 = 100

$\qquad$ GDP deflator$_{99}$ $\qquad$ = (1075) / (740) × 100 = 145.27

$\qquad$ Percentage change = (145.27 − 100)/100 = 45.27%

The percentage change in the GDP deflator is not identical to that of the CPI calculated in problem 3 since the two indices use different quantity weights.

Analytical Questions

2. No, you cannot conclude that the standard of living in the developed country is 17 times that of the developing country. GDP per capita is an imperfect estimate of the standard of living. For example, GDP does not include activities that take place outside of formal markets, such as home-grown agricultural produce. Non-market activities are probably far more important in the developing country than they are in the developed economy, so GDP per capita does a *worse* job estimating the standard of living in the developing country. On the other hand, GDP does not include any measurement of environmental quality—which could be very different across countries, and would certainly impact the quality of life in each case.

    There are certain to be many other examples of differences between the two economies that are not captured by GDP accounting. These many differences make it impossible to state that the individuals in one country are "17 times better off" than the individuals in the other country.

Chapter 6: Fiscal Policy, Saving, and Growth

Review Questions

2. There are three ways that a government can finance its expenditures: by taxing, by selling bonds (deficit finance), or by printing money. In the United States it is illegal for the government to print money to directly finance government spending.

4. The *government intertemporal budget constraint* (GIBC) is written as follows:

$$B_t + \frac{G_t}{R_t} + \frac{G_{t+1}}{R_t R_{t+1}} + \cdots = \frac{Z_t}{R_t} + \frac{Z_{t+1}}{R_t R_{t+1}} + \cdots$$

In words, we are saying that the current stock of debt (B_t) plus the present value of all future government spending must equal the present value of all future net tax receipts.
Fiscal policy decisions do not occur in a vacuum since they must be considered in terms of the GIBC. For example, if government spending is increased at time t, then there must be an offsetting change in either future government spending (decrease) or future net tax receipts (increase) in order for the GIBC to remain balanced.

6. A *generational account* is a measure of the present value of all net taxes (taxes minus transfers) paid by an individual over his or her lifetime.
If a $100 tax is imposed on a young person, that person's generational account is equal to $100. If, on the other hand, the $100 tax is imposed on the person when he or she is old, then the value of the generational account is equal to the present value of that future tax payment, or $100/(1+r)$, which is a smaller value.
On average, young people have positive net taxes since they pay taxes during their working years and receive relatively little by way of transfers. Older people, however, pay less in taxes, receive more transfers, and generally have negative net taxes.

8. A *payroll tax* is a tax levied on income from wages and salaries. In the life-cycle model, payroll taxes fall on the young. A *consumption tax* is a tax on the amount consumed by an individual. In this chapter, we have assumed that the young save all of their wages and consume nothing (that is, $\alpha = 0$). Under these assumptions, the consumption tax would fall entirely on the elderly. If

young people also consume ($\alpha > 0$), then the consumption tax would affect both generations.

The payroll tax would shift the transition curve down by the amount taxed away from the young (who would have saved it otherwise). The imposition of a payroll tax will thus decrease the steady state levels of the capital-labor ratio, output, and consumption.

Since the consumption tax falls entirely on the elderly (assuming $\alpha = 0$), it will have no effect on the transition curve or the steady-state variables, but will directly decrease the amount consumed by the elderly.

10. The *Social Security system* includes *Old Age and Survivors Insurance* (the basic Social Security benefit for retirees and surviving spouses), *Disability Insurance* (a benefit for younger workers who become disabled), and *Medicare* (health care coverage for the elderly).

In the United States, Social Security has historically been financed on a *pay-as-you-go* basis. That is, workers pay taxes on wages and salaries which are then used to pay *current* social security benefits to retirees.

A $4,000 Social Security benefit when old *would not* offset $4,000 in Social Security taxes in the generational account. Since the benefit would not be received at the same time the taxes are paid, the benefit must be discounted to the present, causing the generational account to increase.

12. Examples of *government capital formation* include (but are not limited to) investment in roads, schools, hospitals, public universities, sewer systems, libraries, jails, etc. Although a great deal of government spending goes to government consumption, expenditures on investment improve the productive capacity of the economy as a whole, and can be considered part of the aggregate capital stock. The new transition equation is written:

$$k_{t+1} = A \left(1 - \beta\right) k_t^{\beta} - f_t + k^g_{t+1}$$

Therefore, government investment financed by taxes on the young would not affect the transition path if $f_t = k^g_{t+1}$.

14. *Intragenerational transfers* (a *safety net* for the poor) will affect capital formation if the individuals involved save at different rates. For example, the very poor may have very low saving rates (high α), while the relatively wealthy may have higher saving rates (low α). In that case, if the wealthy are taxed to provide intragenerational transfers to the poor, overall saving will fall, leading to lower capital accumulation. If, on the other hand, the transfers are made from low savers to high savers, it will lead to greater capital accumulation.

In addition, the existence of a social safety net may lead to lower levels of *precautionary saving* (putting aside funds for unexpected needs), which would reduce total capital accumulation.

Numerical Questions

2. a. For the old generation immediately following the change in tax policy: they were required to pay $40, but were not required to pay the $60 when they were young. Thus, their generational account is just equal to $40.

    b. For the young generation immediately following the change in tax policy: they were required to pay $60 when young plus $40 when old. Their generational account will equal the *present value* of their total tax payments = $60 + $40/(1+2) = $60 + $13.33 = $73.33.

    c. generational account of the old = $70
        generational account of the young = $30 + $70/(1+2) = $53.33
        This version of the tax system increases the generational account of an old individual and decreases the account of a young individual.

4. a.

Period	k	r
0	4.3531	0.4286
1	1.3531	0.9711
2	0.0659	8.0531

    b. The generational account is equal to $3 in each period.

    c. Financing government expenditures with bonds that are paid back (with interest) the next period will make no difference. Young people will still turn over $3 to the government that they would have used for capital otherwise. Since the old people will be taxed to cover the repayment of the bonds, the generational account will still be $3 (the present value of the tax on the old people = [$3(1+r)]/(1+r) = $3). Therefore, the capital-labor ratios will be the same as in part a.

    d. Since the capital-labor ratios are unchanged from part a, the interest rate values are unchanged as well.

tax collected (per person) in period 1 = \$3(1+r) = \$3(1.9711) = \$5.91
tax collected (per person) in period 2 = \$3(1+r) = \$3(9.0531) = \$27.16

Analytical Questions

2. For the GIBC to be satisfied, it is equivalent to either pay off the debt (at any point in time) or to pay interest on it forever. Since the size of the debt itself is constant, there is no fear that the debt will "explode," violating the GIBC. If we let B/N equal the amount of bonds sold to each young person, then they each will be repaid $(B/N)(1+r)$ when the bonds mature (when they are old), but they will also be taxed $(B/N)r$ to pay for the interest on the debt. The generational account is the present value of net tax payments:

    generational account = $((B/N)r)/(1+r)$

The steady-state capital-labor ratio will be reduced because some of the savings of the young will be held as bonds instead of capital.
This financing scheme is similar to pay-as-you-go Social Security in that the young "pay" the government a certain amount when they are young, then they are "paid" back the same amount when they are old. Here, the young pay in the amount B/N. The net amount that each will be repaid equals $(B/N)(1+r)-(B/N)r = B/N$. Unlike pay-as-you-go Social Security, this story started off with the need to finance government spending, not as a way to ensure that individuals save for retirement.

Chapter 7: Money and Prices in the Closed Economy

Review Questions

2. *Money* is anything that is widely accepted as a means of payment. We expect any form of money to perform the following three functions: it should serve as a *medium of exchange*, it should serve as a *store of value*, and it should act as a *unit of account*. M1 is the most narrow measure of the money supply calculated by the Federal Reserve. It includes the value of currency held by the public plus the value of all demand deposits.

4. The three functions of money are that it serves as a *medium of exchange*, it serves as a *store of value*, and it acts as a *unit of account*. In acting as a medium of exchange, money makes the economy more efficient by allowing individuals to make transactions without having to resort to barter. Since barter requires a "double coincidence of wants," transactions are very costly. By acting as a store of value, money holds its value over time and serves as a financial asset. By acting as a unit of account, money increases economic efficiency by providing an easy way to state the value of goods and services, as well as a way to keep track of deferred payments and other types of contracts.

6. The *quantity equation* is written:

   $$Mv = PY$$

   where M is equal to the money supply, v is the velocity of money, P is the price level, and Y is real income.
   The *quantity theory of money* is derived from the quantity equation by assuming that velocity is constant ($\bar{v}$), and by further assuming that Y is independent of the money supply and the price level. Thus, an increase in the money supply will lead to an equal proportionate increase in the price level.

8. The *opportunity cost* of holding money is the nominal interest rate, which is equal to the real interest rate plus the inflation rate. By choosing to hold money (which is assumed to earn no interest—for example as currency held in your pocket), an individual gives up the interest that he or she could have earned by holding real assets (capital). The return on capital, however, is the real interest rate. As the individual holds money over time, its value is eroded by inflation (or enhanced by deflation). Thus, the total opportunity cost is the foregone real interest plus the loss of value caused by inflation.
   The *lifetime budget constraint* when individuals hold money is the following:

$$\frac{c_{ot+1}}{(1+r_{t+1})} + \frac{i_{t+1}}{(1+i_{t+1})}\frac{m_{t+1}}{P_t} = w_t$$

10. The *transition equation* with money is written as follows:

$$k_{t+1} = (1 - \gamma[i_{t+1}])A(1-\beta)k_t^\beta - f_t$$

12. In the text, three cases are presented in which the government adds to the money stock:

Case 1: The government prints money for transfers to the elderly.
In this case, the transfer cannot affect the saving decisions of the young, so it will not affect the path of the capital-labor ratio, or the paths of any other real variables in the model. The old people have more money, but they will only be able to buy the same amount of goods, so they are no better off than they were before. In fact the only result of the transfer is an increase in the price level proportionate to that of the increase in the money supply. Thus, money is neutral.

Case 2: The government prints money to finance its own consumption.
Here the government is buying output from the young. It is immediately clear that if the government is buying some output for its own consumption, then there will be less available for households to consume. Thus, some real variables are affected by the increase in the money supply, and money is not neutral.

Case 3: The government prints money for transfers to the young.
In this case, the young at the time of the transfer receive something of real value—at the expense of the elderly at that time. The fiscal term (*f*) in the transition equation will be negative, and thus capital accumulation will be higher than it would have been otherwise. Therefore, the real values in the model will be changed, and money will not be neutral.

14. Increases in the money supply and inflation may affect the *real fiscal position* of the government through the effects of *seigniorage*, the *reduction of the real value of the government debt*, *bracket creep*, and *decreased real government spending*.

Seigniorage (or the "inflation tax") is a measure of the real resources that the government acquires by printing money.

Reduction of the real value of the government debt takes place when surprise inflation causes the nominal interest rates on the government debt to be lower than they would have been if the inflation had been expected.

Bracket creep is a term that describes the situation when an economy uses a progressive income tax system (higher income levels are taxed at higher marginal tax rates) in which the tax brackets are not indexed for inflation. Thus, inflation causes nominal incomes to "creep" into higher tax brackets, leading to higher government tax revenue.

Decreased real government spending occurs when various government expenditures are not indexed for inflation (the nominal values are fixed), and their real values deteriorate as the price level rises.

Numerical Questions

2. a. The capital-labor ratio is calculated using the transition equation with γ fixed at the value 0.1 (no fiscal policy):

$$k_{t+1} = (1-\bar{\gamma})A(1-\beta)k_t^\beta$$

Per capita earnings are given by:

$$w_t = A(1-\beta)k_t^\beta$$

The price level is calculated using the following equation:

$$P_t = \frac{\overline{M}}{\bar{\gamma}w_t N}$$

Period	k	w	P
0	2.0000	4.3090	23.2072
1	3.8781	5.2560	19.0259
2	4.7304	5.5788	17.9252
3	5.0209	5.6794	17.6075
4	5.1115	5.7099	17.5133

b. The steady-state values of the variables are the following:

$$\bar{k} = [(1-\bar{\gamma})A(1-\beta)]^{\frac{1}{1-\beta}} = [(0.9)(5)(0.7)]^{\frac{1}{0.7}} = 5.1508$$

$$\bar{w} = A(1-\beta)k_t^{\beta} = (5)(0.7)(5.1508)^{0.3} = 5.7231$$

$$\bar{P} = \frac{\bar{M}}{\bar{\gamma}\bar{w}N} = \frac{1000}{(0.1)(5.7231)(100)} = 17.4731$$

4. a. Compute the following steady-state values:

     i.   Real money holdings per person:

$$\frac{m}{\bar{P}} = \frac{\bar{M}}{N\bar{P}} = \frac{1000}{(100)(6.4867)} = 1.5416$$

     ii.   Real interest rate:

$$\bar{r} = A\beta\bar{k}^{\beta-1} = (5)(0.3)(3.5971)^{-0.7} = 0.6122$$

     iii.   Nominal interest rate:

$$\bar{i} = \bar{r} + \bar{\pi} = 0.6122 + 0 = 0.6122$$

Note that inflation is equal to zero in the steady state since the price level is constant.

     iv.   Consumption by the old:

$$\bar{c}_o = \left(\bar{w} - \frac{\bar{m}}{\bar{P}}\right)(1+\bar{r}) + \frac{\bar{m}}{\bar{P}} = (5.1387 - 1.5416)(1.6122) + 1.5416 = 7.3408$$

    b.   Substituting steady-state values into the lifetime budget constraint, we get:

$$\frac{\bar{c}_o}{(1+\bar{r})} + \frac{\bar{r}}{(1+\bar{r})}\frac{\bar{m}}{\bar{P}} = \bar{w}$$

$$\overline{c}_o = \overline{w}(1+\overline{r}) - \overline{r}\left(\frac{\overline{m}}{\overline{P}}\right) = (5.1387)(1.6122) - (0.6122)(1.5416) = 7.3408$$

which is equal to the answer above.

Analytical Questions

2.   Increased banking technology will generally allow individuals to have greater access to their deposits. The existence of ATMs, credit cards, and debit cards mean that it will be less necessary to carry currency. As in the United States, these developments will decrease the demand for money and will cause the velocity of money to increase as a given monetary stock is used for a greater number of transactions.
      If we consider these changes in light of the life-cycle model, it is clear that decreased demand for money is equivalent to increased demand for real assets (capital) for individual savers. Therefore, a decrease in demand for money holdings will lead to a higher steady-state capital-labor ratio and greater total output.

4.   An old person would prefer the government to tax the young since printing money to finance the transfers would only cause the price level to rise and would not allow the old people to consume anything additional.
      A young person would prefer the government to print money to finance the transfers to the old. If the government uses a tax, the young will have fewer resources to save for their old age. If, on the other hand, the government prints money, the young are no worse off than they were before.

Chapter 8: The Keynesian Model of Price and Wage Rigidity

Review Questions

2. *Nominal rigidity* means that a nominal price is inflexible or "sticky." Some examples of prices that exhibit nominal rigidity include wages in some sectors of the labor market, magazine prices, restaurant prices, any prices controlled by contracts, and many others. Nominal rigidity is more likely to occur in markets that are not highly competitive (that is, a market with either few buyers or few sellers). Contracts in the labor market (for example in union shops) or between suppliers and their customers will also lead to nominal rigidity. Furthermore, some rigidities are legislated, like the federal minimum wage. Price stickiness is generally not symmetric in that prices will usually be free to adjust upwards, but are often sticky downwards. For example, relatively few workers ever receive a pay cut.

4. Keynesians have generally assumed that prices are sticky downward in the short run, but are fully flexible in the short run. This assumption is very important in that it is the basis for the Keynesian explanation of business cycle fluctuations—people become involuntarily unemployed when wages and/or prices fail to adjust adequately. In the life-cycle model, we can incorporate wage or price rigidities by looking only at the short run and fixing either the wage or the price level at some minimum value (we assume that prices are always flexible upwards). In order for the important equations in the model to continue to balance, employment will be allowed to vary.

6. The equation for the IS curve is:

$$Y = \frac{F + \phi[r_{+1}]}{(1 - \beta)(1 - \gamma[r_{+1}])}$$

    Within the IS equation we assume that the parameter β and the fiscal variable F are held constant. In general we assume that A and N are being held constant as well. The IS curve shows us the inverse relationship between total output (Y) and the real interest rate (r).

8. *Monetary policy* is the decision-making process in which the government chooses a value for the nominal money supply ($\overline{M}$). An increase in the nominal money stock will shift the LM curve to the right, increasing output and decreasing the real interest rate. The *multiplier process* means that output will

rise by a greater amount than the increase in the real money stock. When a monetary infusion takes place, output will increase, raising the incomes of both the young (higher employment) and the old (greater use of capital). The old are thus able to consume more and the young are able to accumulate more capital—leading to higher output in the future. The multiplier tells us how much output *would have increased* if the interest rate had not fallen. It is equal to the horizontal distance between the old LM curve and the new LM curve. The multiplier effect is dampened, however, since the higher capital stock will lead to a lower real interest rate—that is, higher output causes a movement along the IS curve to a lower real interest rate.

10. In the *short run*, expansionary monetary policy causes a rightward shift in the LM curve, leading to a higher level of output and a lower real interest rate. This monetary policy will lead to higher investment and consumption. Expansionary fiscal policy causes a rightward shift in the IS curve, and will also yield a higher level of output, but will cause the real interest rate to rise. Fiscal policy will crowd out private investment and reduce private consumption as government consumption increases.
In the *long run*, expansionary monetary policy will cause greater investment, leading to higher output and wages in the future. Fiscal policy, however, reduces the resources available for investment (by giving them to the government), leading to lower output and wages in the future.

12. The interest sensitivity of money demand reduces the effectiveness of monetary policy. The shift in the LM curve leads to higher output and a lower real interest rate. Since money demand is sensitive to the interest rate, young people hold a greater share of their assets as money instead of capital—yielding a smaller increase in aggregate demand and output.
The interest sensitivity of money demand, however, makes fiscal policy more effective. The shift in the IS curve leads to higher output and a higher real interest rate. Money demand by the young will decrease (since the opportunity cost of holding money is higher), and investment will not be completely crowded out by government spending.

14. The *paradox of thrift* occurs when lower private or government consumption causes an increase in national saving (which is a decrease in aggregate demand). The drop in aggregate demand leads to a decrease in total output—thus leading to lower saving overall. It is a paradox in that the attempt to increase saving ultimately can lead to a reduction in saving as the size of the economy declines.

16. *Involuntary unemployment* will occur when a nominal wage rigidity persists through the following mechanism: If the nominal wage is fixed at some minimum value $\overline{W}$ the real wage at the current price level is $\overline{W}/P$. If the market-clearing real wage is less than that value, then some individuals will be unemployed as firms hire the optimal number of workers *given* the current real wage.

18. The *aggregate demand* curve shows the total of all output purchased in the economy at a given price level. In our simplified life-cycle model (young people do not consume), aggregate demand is equal to capital purchases by the young, consumption by the old, and government spending.
The *aggregate supply* curve shows all of the possible combinations of the price level and output that are consistent with labor market equilibrium.
As long as the economy is initially below its full-employment output level, expansionary fiscal or monetary policy will lead to an increase (shift to the right) of the aggregate demand curve. The new equilibrium will have a higher level of output and a higher price level.

Numerical Questions

2. a. After making the changes required by the problem, the equation for the IS curve is:

$$Y = \frac{F + (260/r_{+1})}{(1-\beta)(1-\bar{\gamma})}$$

Y	r_{+1}
750	0.9905
800	0.9286
850	0.8739
900	0.8254
950	0.7820

b. Using the values of r_{+1} calculated above and assuming that $F=10$, we get new values for Y:

r_{+1}	Y'
0.9905	778.57
0.9286	828.57
0.8739	878.57
0.8254	928.57
0.7820	978.57

Clearly, the value of output is higher (by 28.57 units) at each interest rate, so the IS curve must have shifted to the right.

c.   If γ falls to a value of 0.3, we get the following real interest rates corresponding to the output levels given in part a:

Y	r_{+1}
750	0.7075
800	0.6633
850	0.6242
900	0.5896
950	0.5585

The real interest rate is now lower at each income level than it was in part a. Another way to look at it is that at each interest rate on the new IS curve corresponds to a lower output level. Thus, the decrease in γ has caused the IS curve to shift to the left. This result is not surprising since a decrease in the fraction of assets held as money will cause greater capital accumulation and lower real interest rates.

4.   Assuming that $\gamma = 0.5$ for both the IS and LM curves:

Equation for the LM curve:

$$Y = \frac{\overline{M}}{\overline{\gamma}(1 - \beta)\overline{P}}$$

Equation for the IS curve:

$$Y = \frac{F + \phi[r_{+1}]}{(1 - \beta)(1 - \overline{\gamma})} = \frac{F + (260/r_{+1})}{(1 - \beta)(1 - \overline{\gamma})}$$

Setting the two equations equal to each other we get:

$$\frac{\overline{M}}{\overline{\gamma}(1-\beta)\overline{P}} = \frac{F+(260/r_{+1})}{(1-\beta)(1-\overline{\gamma})}$$

$$\frac{297.5}{(0.5)(0.7)(1)} = \frac{0+(260/r_{+1})}{(0.7)(0.5)}$$

$$r_{+1} = \frac{260}{297.5} = 0.8739$$

Substituting this value for r_{+1} back into the IS equation gives us:

$$Y = \frac{F+(260/r_{+1})}{(1-\beta)(1-\overline{\gamma})} = \frac{0+(260/0.8739)}{(0.7)(0.5)} = 850.05$$

b.   The *flexible price* equilibrium is the *steady state* equilibrium:

Solve for the steady-state capital-labor ratio:

$$\overline{k} = [(1-\overline{\gamma})(1-\beta)A]^{\frac{1}{1-\beta}} = [(0.5)(0.7)(4)]^{\frac{1}{0.7}} = 1.6172$$

Use the value for the steady-state capital-labor ratio to solve for total output:

$$\overline{Y} = NA\overline{k}^{\beta} = (200)(4)(1.6172)^{0.3} = 924.09$$

Use the value for the steady-state capital-labor ratio to solve for the real interest rate:

$$\overline{r} = \beta A\overline{k}^{\beta-1} = (0.3)(4)(1.6172)^{-0.7} = 0.8571$$

Note that the flexible prices equilibrium has a higher level of output and a lower real interest rate than that calculated in part a.

c.   There must be unemployment of resources in the equilibrium described in part a since output is below the full-employment level calculated in part b.

d.   The flexible price equilibrium price level is calculated using the equation:

$$P = \frac{\overline{M}}{\overline{\gamma}w_t N} = \frac{\overline{M}}{\overline{\gamma}(1-\beta)A\overline{k}^{\beta}N} = \frac{297.5}{(0.5)(0.7)(4)(1.6172)^{0.3}(200)} = 0.9198$$

Note that this price is below $\overline{P}=1$, so the fixed price level was "too high," causing unemployment.

Analytical Questions

2.   In an economy with rigid prices, the destruction of a large fraction of the money supply would operate much like a *contractionary* monetary policy, that is ΔM would be negative instead of positive. We would expect the LM curve to shift to the left, leading to lower total output and a higher real interest rate. Old people will have less consumption, while young people will have lower income and fewer resources available for saving. The reduction in investment by the young will reduce future output as well.

Chapter 9: Understanding Recessions

Review Questions

2.   In the *traditional Keynesian model*, we can explain the Phillips curve by assuming that nominal wages are rigid and that output is below its full-employment level. We further assume that workers negotiate nominal wage increases that match the inflation rate of the previous period. If the government increases the money supply (or uses expansionary fiscal policy to the same degree) so that inflation will be higher than it was in the past, the real wage will fall and output will increase. In this way the government will use a policy that increases inflation to achieve a lower rate of unemployment.

4.   *Rational expectations* about inflation are formed when individuals use the information available to them (including information about possible government actions) to logically make predictions about the inflation rate in the future. If people make economic decisions based on rational expectations, then the government will be unable to systematically fool them into accepting lower real wages. A short-run Phillips curve may still arise under rational expectations as the result of *unanticipated* shocks to the economy.

6.   The *misperceptions model* has been criticized in that people can easily educate themselves about the economy and the policies of the government, especially regarding the price level. The misperception theorists answer this critique by saying that what they *really* mean is that people need a great deal of very precise information to make accurate predictions about the future. Much of the economic information that is readily available to the public is highly aggregated and frequently revised. Furthermore, households often make long-term decisions (say in buying a house, accepting a job, or starting a business) that rely on difficult long-term predictions of economic conditions. Therefore, in some cases individuals will make poor predictions of the future or will *misperceive* the current economic situation.

8.   The *real business cycle theory* has been criticized in the following ways:
(1) Real shocks are often hard to measure or evaluate.
(2) Since many real shocks are unobservable, we can "explain" any economic fluctuation as the result of an unobserved real shock.
(3) It doesn't seem reasonable to explain the Great Depression or severe recessions as the result of workers choosing to take more leisure in response to a decrease in real wages.

(4) Labor usage fluctuates more over the business cycle than the real business cycle seems to predict.

(5) Technological shocks probably vary across industries and may average out across the entire economy.

Real business cycle theorists answer these criticisms as follows:

(1) Many real shocks *are* observable—examples from the text include natural disasters and changes in trade policy.

(2) Technological breakthroughs may be difficult to measure, but they are often very important.

(3) Even though you *could* try to explain any economic event as the result of various real shocks, the real question should focus on whether the theory can explain a great deal of macroeconomic fluctuation using a reasonable set of real shocks.

(4) Much of the blame for the Great Depression can be assigned to the collapse (or near collapse) of the U.S. banking system. The dearth of credit availability led to many business failures. We can view this series of events as a real shock to productivity that resulted in very low wages.

(5) Employees don't vary their labor supply as much as is predicted by the model because employers frequently require full-time work and lay off excess workers during recessions.

(6) Industry-specific shocks may be correlated, thereby producing an aggregate shock.

10. The *sectoral shift model* has been criticized in the following ways:

(1) People often change jobs *in response to recessions*—not as a cause of recessions.

(2) If recessions reflect changes in the composition of demand, then periods of high unemployment should be coincident with periods of high job vacancy rates—but the opposite is true.

Sectoral shift theorists respond to the criticisms as follows:

(1) It may be impossible to determine the cause of a specific recession since some may be caused by aggregate shocks and others may be caused by interindustry variations.

(2) The unemployment rate-job vacancy rate relationship is not stable over time—possibly due to sectoral shifts.

(3) Job mobility rises during recessions.

12. Robert Barro examined the effects of anticipated and unanticipated monetary shocks on U.S. output. Barro found a fairly close correlation between unanticipated money shocks and shocks to output, and very little correlation

between anticipated money shocks and shocks to output. Some critics of Barro's work have pointed out that there are other ways to divide money supply changes into the categories of "anticipated" or "unanticipated," and these other approaches could lead to differing results. Moreover, Barro's research may have been flawed by his neglect of the *timing* of monetary shocks—if a monetary shock takes place after contracts have been finalized, then individuals may not be able to fully respond to this "anticipated" change in the money supply.

14. The theory of *political business cycles* states that politicians have an incentive to use expansionary fiscal and/or monetary policy immediately prior to an election since voters will give great consideration to the current state of the economy. After the election, the policies may well be reversed, leading to an economic contraction.

    In a traditional Keynesian model, we would see the politicians as using policy to increase aggregate demand (shift the AD curve to the right). After the election, the AD curve would shift back, reducing output and employment.

    In a real business cycle model, tax cuts could lead to additional labor supply and greater output. After the elections, an increase in taxes would reverse the movement of labor supply and reduce output.

Numerical Questions

2. a. The value of A_t drops from a maximum of 6 to a minimum of 4, which is a 33.3% drop. The largest percentage drop in total output is 28.8%. Since the capital-labor ratio is determined in the prior period, the capital-labor ratio will *rise* at the same time A_t *drops* from 6 to 4—thus Y_t will not fall as much as it would have if the capital-labor ratio is constant.

    b. Changes in consumption from period to period move in the same direction as those of output, but have smaller magnitudes (they are "dampened"). Thus the model described in this problem is consistent with the idea of consumption smoothing.

Analytical Questions

2. With very high inflation rates we would expect to see more frequent price changes since firms have more to lose by waiting than they would in periods of low inflation. An example of this behavior was presented in chapter 8 (*Case*

Study: U.S. Magazine Prices). In Stephen Cecchetti's research on magazine pricing, he found that publishers changed their prices much more frequently when the inflation rate was relatively high.

Chapter 10: The Nature and Costs of Unemployment

Review Questions

2.   The *labor force participation rate* is the ratio of the number of adults who are in the labor force (either employed or unemployed) to the number of adults in the population. *Discouraged workers* are individuals who were unemployed, but gave up looking for work, and thus dropped out of the labor force. Discouraged workers are *not* counted as unemployed. These concepts were introduced in chapter 4. During recessions, unemployed people will find it harder to become employed, and they may drop out of the labor force. During economic expansions, individuals will find it easier to become employed, and those who were not previously in the labor force may start looking for work or find a job. Thus the labor force participation rate will go up during expansions and down during recessions.

4.   *Gross flows* describe the total number of individuals entering or leaving a particular labor market state. For example, the total of all people newly employed would be a gross flow into employment. *Net flows* describe the total number of individuals entering a particular labor market state *minus* the total number of individuals leaving that state. For example, the number of people newly employed (or *accessions*) minus the number of people who have left employment (or *separations*), is the net inflow to employment. When net flows to employment are negative, more people are separating than are being hired.

6.   In terms of gross flows, it is true that "small business is the engine of job creation," in that small businesses are responsible for a large proportion of all new jobs created. If we consider the net flows into employment, we see that small businesses are also responsible for a large proportion of lost jobs since small businesses are relatively more likely to go out of business or contract in size.

8.   The *duration* of unemployment is generally measured in terms of the weeks spent unemployed. During recessions, duration usually increases as individuals find it harder to find new jobs. *Long-term unemployment* is generally defined as an unemployment spell lasting at least 15 weeks.

10.   The *efficiency wage theory* claims that firms will set their wages above the equilibrium wage in order to get workers to work harder or more carefully (more efficiently), especially if the workers cannot be easily monitored. The key idea is that if the workers are caught *shirking* they will be fired. If fired, the

workers will face the task of finding a new job (probably at the lower equilibrium wage), or they may remain unemployed. The efficiency wage process will contribute to unemployment because firms that pay a higher real wage will necessarily hire fewer workers, since they will still require that the real wage equal the last worker's marginal product.

12. *Frictional unemployment* occurs when people are temporarily between jobs, or when a new entrant to the labor force is looking for employment. We do not necessarily expect frictional unemployment to be higher or lower than usual during recessions since there will always be people changing jobs or entering the labor force in the economy. The sectoral shift model predicts that the expansions and contractions of different sectors of the economy will *cause* some recessions, further predicting a rise in frictional unemployment.

14. The *private costs* of unemployment primarily consist of wages lost by the former worker. The *social costs* of unemployment consist of the output that could have been produced if the worker were still employed.
Reduced output may *overstate* the social costs of unemployment since the unemployed people may still do productive things—they may work around the house, care for their children, or participate in other types of *home production*. If people choose to become unemployed (they are voluntarily unemployed), we know that they must as individuals value what they can now accomplish or they would not have quit their jobs in the first place.
Reduced output may *understate* the social costs of unemployment in that it does not include any of the social problems that often accompany high unemployment rates—more crime, more family problems, etc.

16. *Okun's Law* is an empirical relationship between changes in the unemployment rate and the annual growth rate of real GDP that was first observed by Arthur Okun. The "law" shows that for every one percentage point decrease in the unemployment rate we would (on average) expect about a two percent increase in the growth rate of real GDP. The growth accounting equation is:

$$\Delta Y/Y = \Delta A/A + \beta \, \Delta K/K + (1-\beta) \, \Delta L/L$$

We can estimate that a one percent decrease in unemployment is roughly equal to a one percent increase in labor input, but $(1-\beta) \, \Delta L/L$ is too small to account for the relationship that Okun observed. We also know, however, that multifactor productivity is procyclical—so we would also expect to see an increase in A at a time when we see decreased unemployment.

18. *Hysteresis* occurs when changes in the actual unemployment rate lead to an adjustment of the natural rate of unemployment. If government policies are effective in reducing the number of long-term unemployed people, for example, then the natural rate of unemployment may be reduced.

Numerical Questions

2. a. In any given month during the year, two people out of 50 are unemployed, therefore the unemployment rate = 2/50 = 4%

   b. In a given month, half of the unemployment is short-term, and half is long-term. If we consider the year as a whole, 12/13 = 92% of unemployment is short-term, and 1/13 = 8% is long-term. These percentages are different from those in part a because of the timing of the calculation. If we are considering monthly unemployment, we only consider the labor flows, for that month. If we are considering the whole year, however, we will count the twelve *different* people who were each unemployed for one month.

   c. monthly unemployment rate = 4/63 = 6.35%
      The cloned people will increase the unemployment rate since the number of unemployed people in a given month doubled, but the labor force rose by a smaller percentage.

   d. monthly unemployment rate = 3/50 = 6%
      The increase in duration has increased the unemployment rate compared to that in part a since there are now three individuals who are unemployed in a given month.

Analytical Questions

2. While there is fairly strong evidence that unemployment insurance programs lead to greater unemployment, there may be some benefits to society from unemployment of this type. One benefit mentioned in the text, is that workers may be willing to take more "risks" by accepting jobs in volatile industries if they know that there is a social safety net. Another possible benefit stems from the increased duration of unemployment that appears to correspond to the unemployment insurance benefits. If workers remain unemployed for a longer period of time (instead of accepting the first possible job prospect), they may find a better job that increases their long-term productivity.

Chapter 11: Countercyclical Policy

Review Questions

2.   From 1929 through early 1933, GDP was falling as the United States entered
      the Great Depression. After the beginning of 1933, output began to grow, but
      didn't regain its 1929 level until 1936. Output again dropped during the 1937-
      38 recession, and then resumed its pattern of growth.

4.   The *stance of fiscal policy* is much harder to measure than the results of fiscal
      policy since the state of the economy will affect what actually happens.
      Because of the existence of *automatic stabilizers*, tax revenue tends to fall
      during recessions and increase during expansions. On the other hand, certain
      types of government spending (especially transfers) tend to increase during
      recessions and decrease during expansions. Thus, government spending and
      tax revenue will fluctuate with the business cycle—not just with changes in
      policy.
      In order to avoid the confusion that is described above, policy makers can use a
      tool called the *full-employment budget deficit*—an estimate of what the deficit
      would be if the economy were producing at full employment.

6.   Policy makers face many of the following *uncertainties*:
      -   They probably don't know where the economy is in the business cycle since
          the data is often hard to interpret until well after the beginning of a
          recession or an expansion.
      -   If a certain policy is implemented, policy makers will not be certain as to
          how long it will take to reach its full effectiveness.
      -   Even if policy makers know that the economy is in a recession (or entering
          one), they may not know what has caused the recession or what the best
          remedy would be.

8.   A *dynamically inconsistent policy* is one in which the government has a strong
      incentive to change an announced policy after the public has already reacted to
      it. Policy makers in the government can overcome dynamic inconsistency
      through *precommitment*—that is, by stating ahead of time that they will give up
      the opportunity to change the announced policy. For example, an independent
      central bank (like the U.S. Federal Reserve) removes monetary policy from the
      hands of the President and Congress.

10.   *Incomes policies* are an attempt by the government to control inflation by
      assessing financial penalties to firms that raise prices or wages. As in the

example in the text, policy makers may wish to move the economy to a lower rate of inflation. Assuming that the government adopts a monetary policy consistent with the adopted incomes policy, then it is likely that inflation will drop more quickly than it would otherwise. By encouraging businesses not to raise wages and prices, the government gains time for individuals to realize that the inflation rate has fallen—and for them to adjust their expectations of future inflation downward.

Analytical Questions

2. "The introduction of wage and price controls is likely to give rise to a black market for various goods and services." The statement above implies that individuals will go to great lengths to evade regulations that do not make economic "sense." When prices and wages are fully flexible they adjust to changes in supply and/or demand. When the prices and wages *do not* adjust to these changes, we will see situations where an excess demand (shortage) or excess supply (surplus) develops. If prices are absolutely fixed at their initial nominal values, either situation can lead to the development of a black market—surplus goods will be sold below the official price and shortage goods will be sold above the official price. If, instead, prices are capped at their initial nominal values (and allowed to adjust downward), then no excess supply will arise. The existence of black markets will move the actual prices closer to the flexible price equilibrium, but at the cost of significant illegal activity.

Chapter 12: Saving and Growth in the International Economy

Review Questions

2. *Net foreign investment* is the difference between national saving and domestic investment. A country can invest abroad by either exporting capital to the other country, or by exporting consumption goods, selling them, and using the proceeds to purchase capital goods in the foreign country.

4. For two countries that are similar *except* for their time preference parameter α:

    World transition equation:
    $$k_{t+1} = (1-\overline{\alpha})(1-\beta)Ak_t^{\beta}$$

    world-wide α:
    $$\overline{\alpha} = \frac{N\alpha + N^*\alpha^*}{N + N^*}$$

    If the two countries are even the same size, the transition equation will be the same, but the world-wide α changes to:

    world-wide α:
    $$\overline{\alpha} = \frac{N(\alpha + \alpha^*)}{2N} = \frac{\alpha + \alpha^*}{2}$$

6. *Factor price equalization* is the equalization of the prices of the factors of production (the real interest rate and the real wage) across countries. Factor price equalization takes place as a result of international trade and investment in the following way:
    Assume that two countries begin trading, but one country (the "home" country) has a higher capital-labor ratio than the other (the "foreign" country). It must be true that the country with the higher capital-labor ratio also has a lower real interest rate since capital is relatively more plentiful than it is in the other country. Owners of capital in the home country would therefore prefer to invest some of their assets in the foreign country and receive a higher rate of return. When this foreign investment occurs, the home country capital-labor ratio will fall (and the foreign country value of k will rise), and the home country real interest rate will rise (and the foreign country value of r will fall). Eventually, each country will have the same capital-labor ratio, and thus the same real interest rate. Furthermore, if both countries have the same capital-labor ratio, they must also have the same real wage rate.

The empirical evidence for factor price equalization shows that the real interest rates of similar industrialized countries do tend to move in the same direction, but they are not identical—perhaps because of differing mistakes in forecasting the inflation rate. It is very difficult to compare real wage rates since they are stated in terms of local currencies (and thus must be compared using exchange rates), and must be adjusted for skill levels, work conditions, etc.

8. Under *autarky*, the *net foreign asset position* of a low-saving country (or any country, for that matter) will be equal to zero. Under *free trade*, the low-saving country will be receiving capital from the high-saving country, so its net foreign asset position will be negative.

10. If a low-saving country's government chooses to *restrict foreign trade* there will be clear winners and losers: the winners are the old at the time of the new trade policy since they will receive a higher real interest rate on their assets. Those who are young at the time the new policy is implemented (and all future generations who face the same policy) lose because they have less capital to work with, earn lower real wages, and generate less output. We would see the opposite result for trade restrictions in a high-saving country.

12. It is very easy to modify our open-economy model to show the effects of fiscal policy. The world-wide transition curve is modified in the same way that we changed the individual country's transition curve—by subtracting a fiscal term that shows resources taken from the young.

World transition equation with fiscal policy:

$$k_{t+1} = (1-\overline{\alpha})(1-\beta)Ak_t^\beta - \overline{f}$$

world-wide fiscal term:

$$\overline{f} = \frac{Nf + N^*f^*}{N + N^*}$$

Numerical Questions

2. a. Under autarky, it is impossible for the countries to hold assets abroad, so their *net foreign asset positions* must equal zero.

   b. In each country, the steady-state capital stock will equal the common capital-labor ratio times the number of workers in that country.

Savum: $K = N\bar{k} = (100)(1.7171) = 171.71$

Spendum: $K = N\bar{k} = (200)(1.7171) = 343.41$

c.   Total assets owned by each country depends on saving by individuals in that country:

Savum: $N\bar{a} = N(1-\alpha)\bar{w} = (100)(0.7)(3.4342) = 240.39$

Spendum: $N\bar{a} = N(1-\alpha)\bar{w} = (200)(0.4)(3.4342) = 274.74$

d.   The net foreign asset position of each country is the difference between the amount of assets that are owned by each country and the capital used within the country:

Savum: $N\bar{a} - K = 240.39 - 171.71 = 68.68$

Spendum: $N\bar{a} - K = 274.74 - 343.41 = -68.67$

e.   Yes, the results are what we expect. Under autarky, countries do not trade, and thus will not invest internationally. Under free trade, we expect Savum (the high-saving country) to invest in Spendum (the low-saving country) in order to achieve a higher rate of return on assets.

4.   a.   Calculate steady-state consumption per old person and per young person for each country under autarky:

Savum: $\bar{c}_o = (1-\alpha)\bar{w}(1+\bar{r}) = (0.7)(3.8417)(1.4762) = 3.9698$

$\bar{c}_y = \alpha\bar{w} = (0.3)(3.8417) = 1.1525$

Spendum: $\bar{c}_o = (1-\alpha)\bar{w}(1+\bar{r}) = (0.4)(3.1880)(1.8333) = 2.3378$

$\bar{c}_y = \alpha\bar{w} = (0.6)(3.1880) = 1.9128$

b.   Steady-state utility in each country:

Savum: $\quad \bar{u} = (\bar{c}_y)^\alpha (\bar{c}_o)^{(1-\alpha)} = (1.1525)^{0.3} (3.9698)^{0.7} = 2.7392$

Spendum: $\quad \bar{u} = (\bar{c}_y)^\alpha (\bar{c}_o)^{(1-\alpha)} = (1.9128)^{0.6} (2.3378)^{0.4} = 2.0726$

c. Steady-state consumption under free trade:

Savum: $\quad \bar{c}_o = (1-\alpha)\bar{w}(1+\bar{r}) = (0.7)(3.4342)(1.6667) = 4.0066$

$\quad\quad\quad\quad \bar{c}_y = \alpha\bar{w} = (0.3)(3.4342) = 1.0303$

Spendum: $\quad \bar{c}_o = (1-\alpha)\bar{w}(1+\bar{r}) = (0.4)(3.4342)(1.6667) = 2.2895$

$\quad\quad\quad\quad \bar{c}_y = \alpha\bar{w} = (0.6)(3.4342) = 2.0605$

In Savum, individuals will consume less when young and more when old under free trade. In Spendum, individuals will consume more when young and less when old under free trade. These differences make sense because in Savum, the real interest rate has gone up (and the real wage fallen) and in Spendum, the real interest rate has fallen (and the real wage has gone up).

d. Steady-state utility under free trade:

Savum: $\quad \bar{u} = (\bar{c}_y)^\alpha (\bar{c}_o)^{(1-\alpha)} = (1.0303)^{0.3} (4.0066)^{0.7} = 2.6658$

Spendum: $\quad \bar{u} = (\bar{c}_y)^\alpha (\bar{c}_o)^{(1-\alpha)} = (2.0605)^{0.6} (2.2895)^{0.4} = 2.1492$

For the people of Savum, individual utility is lower under free trade than it was under autarky. For the people of Spendum, individual utility is increased under free trade. Note that overall utility is equal to 696.42 under free trade versus 688.44 under autarky. Therefore it is possible that the winners (those in Spendum) could pay off the losers (in Savum) so that everyone is made better off through trade. In the real world, however, such payments would be very unlikely. It may help to remember that the individuals in Savum were pursuing higher real returns when they began investing in Spendum. As in many other cases, what was initially beneficial for an individual did not benefit everyone in that economy in the long run.

Analytical Questions

2.   If the two countries are not trading (autarky) then the gift of capital from the high-saving country to the low-saving country will temporarily shift each country away from its individual steady-state capital-labor ratio. The underdeveloped country will see a temporary improvement in its standard of living, but then it will converge back to its original steady state.

     If, on the other hand, the two countries are trading, the gift of capital will raise the capital-labor ratio in the low-saving country and decrease the capital-labor ratio in the high-saving country. Since this change will cause the interest rate in the donor country to increase, the capital will flow back as individuals invest where they will receive the higher return. Again, the change is only temporary. Ultimately, the gift of capital does not change the behavior of the individuals in either country—so the steady state will not change either.

Chapter 13: Money, Exchange Rates, and Policy in the Open Economy

Review Questions

2. A country's currency *appreciates* when its value increases in terms of another currency. For example if the yen per dollar exchange rate increases, then we say that the dollar has appreciated in terms of the yen.
A country's currency *depreciates* when its value falls in terms of another currency. For example if the yen per dollar exchange rate falls, then we say that the dollar has depreciated in terms of the yen.

4. A country's currency is *devalued* when the government sets its fixed exchange rate at a lower value in terms of foreign currency. For example, if the exchange rate is fixed at 100 yen per dollar, the U.S. government could devalue the currency by setting the new exchange rate at 90 yen per dollar.
A country's currency is *revalued* when the government increases the fixed exchange rate in terms of foreign currency (the opposite of a devaluation).

6. Countries that fix the value of a particular commodity in terms of their money are said to be on a *commodity standard*. For example, the United States might agree to buy or sell silver for $20 per ounce. If two countries fix their currencies to the same commodity, they are indirectly adopting a fixed exchange rate for the two currencies. In the past, gold has been used as the commodity standard for fixed exchange rates.

8. The *nominal exchange rate* is the number of units of a foreign country's currency that can be purchased with one unit of the home country's currency. The *real exchange rate* is the ratio of the price of a fixed basket of goods and services in the domestic economy to the price (in terms of domestic currency) of the same basket in a foreign country. The real exchange rate is given by the equation:

$$e^R = \frac{P}{P^*/e}$$

The real exchange rate is sometimes called the *terms of trade*.

10. Assuming constant and equal money demand parameters and factor price equalization, the nominal exchange rate is determined by the equation:

$$e = \frac{M^* / N^*}{M / N}$$

If the domestic money supply rises faster than the foreign money supply, then the exchange rate (in terms of foreign currency per unit of domestic currency) must depreciate.

12. A country cannot choose *both* the exchange rate and the money supply because the two are related by the equation:

$$e = \frac{M^* / N^*}{M / N}$$

If M is chosen according to some monetary policy, then e will be determined by the equation, given values of M^* and N^*. Similarly, if the government tries to fix the exchange rate (e), then the money supply (M) must be adjusted to facilitate that goal.

14. Government *intervention* in the foreign exchange market takes place when the central bank buys or sells currency in order to influence a floating exchange rate.

16. The open economy IS curve is flatter than the closed economy version since the interest rate is determined on the world market. Thus a much larger change in income is required to change the interest rate by a given amount. If the IS curve is completely flat, the small country will not be able to increase output and employment at all using fiscal policy. Monetary policy, however, will be *more* effective in an open economy because there will be no change in the interest rate.

Numerical Questions

2. a. Compute the real exchange rate for each year:

$$e^R = \frac{P}{P^* / e}$$

Year	e (¥/$)	e^R (¥/$)
1987	144.60	156.59
1988	128.17	143.45
1989	138.07	158.52
1990	145.00	170.12
1991	134.59	159.40

The text states that if purchasing power parity held for all goods and services in the basket, then the dollar cost of the basket in Japan should be equal to the dollar cost of the basket in the United States. If purchasing power parity holds, we would expect changes in price levels to cause appropriate changes in the nominal exchange rate (e), leaving the real exchange rate (e^R) unchanged. In the table above, the real exchange rate is not constant.

b.   In this example we see the nominal and real exchange rates generally moving in the same direction—an increase in the nominal exchange rate causes an increase in the real exchange rate. Since both the U.S. and Japanese economies produce many non-traded goods and services, we would actually be surprised if purchasing power parity held perfectly.

Analytical Questions

2.   a.   Calculate the bb/BB purchasing power parity exchange rate (we are considering Big to be the "foreign" country):

$$e = \frac{P^*}{P} = \frac{150}{100} = 1.5 \, \text{bb/BB}$$

According to our calculations, the exchange rate is fixed exactly at the purchasing power parity exchange rate, so there is no need for realignment.

b.   If the price level in Big falls to 125, then the new purchasing power parity exchange rate is given by:

$$e = \frac{P^*}{P} = \frac{125}{100} = 1.25 \, \text{bb/BB}$$

The purchasing power parity exchange rate has fallen because of the increase in value of bigbucks—the same quantity of goods and services can be purchased with fewer bigbucks than before.

c.   With the drop in prices in Big, the fixed exchange rate now undervalues the bigbuck—that is, people in Bigger get more bigbucks per biggerbuck than they should according to purchasing power parity.

d.   Since the bigbuck is undervalued, currency traders will assume that a realignment will eventually take place. In order to take advantage of the situation, speculators will use biggerbucks (BB) to buy bigbucks (bb). Eventually, the Bigger government will run out of bigbucks (its "foreign reserves"), the exchange rate will drop, and the currency traders will be able to take their profits by selling the bigbucks at the new exchange rate. For example:

(1) buy 100 BB worth of bb at the rate of 1.5 bb/BB = 150 bb

(2) sell 150 bb at the new exchange rate of 1.25 bb/BB = 120 BB

(3) profit = 120 BB − 100 BB = 20 BB

4.   In order for the common European currency (the *euro*) to be successful, the participating countries must relinquish their monetary authority to the new European central bank. In other words, the participating countries will be completely unable to use monetary policy to stimulate their economies. Given the text's discussion of the impotence of fiscal policy in small open economies, these countries will be very limited in the tools that they will have available to fight recessions. In the event that a severe recession develops in one member country there may be political repercussions to allowing monetary policy to be controlled by "outsiders" with a larger regional focus.

Chapter 14: The Banking System, the Federal Reserve, and the Money Supply

Review Questions

2. The most liquid assets held by financial institutions include the reserves held as cash, as well as reserves held on deposit at the Fed or deposited in other banks. The most liquid liabilities held by financial intermediaries are demand deposits, since they may be withdrawn "on demand." *Owners' equity* will be negative if the bank's liabilities (excluding owners' equity) outweigh its assets.

4. The *monetary base* consists of bank reserves plus currency held by the public. The formula for the *M1 money multiplier* is:

$$\text{M1 money multiplier} = \frac{M1}{MB} = \frac{cd+1}{cd+rd}$$

If people *do not* hold currency, the formula reduces to:

$$\text{M1 money multiplier (no currency)} = \frac{1}{rd}$$

Therefore, if people hold currency the value of the M1 money multiplier will fall. The intuition behind this change is that currency held by the public is not available for banks to use in the deposit creation process. Thus a given change in the monetary base (MB) will lead to a smaller change in the money supply (M1).

6. The Fed's *Board of Governors* is made up of seven governors who are appointed by the President for staggered 14-year terms. The President also chooses one governor to serve as chairman for a four-year term.
The *Federal Open Market Committee* (FOMC) consists of the seven members of the board of governors, the president of the New York Federal Reserve Bank, and a rotating set of four presidents of the other 11 regional Federal Reserve Banks.

8. Government borrowing is *monetized* when the U.S. Treasury sells new government bonds to the public to pay for current expenditures, and then the Fed purchases those bonds from the public. The Fed can actually issue new currency to pay for the bonds, or (more commonly) it can pay for the bonds by

a check drawn on itself. Monetization occurs when the Fed and the U.S. Treasury are *independently* pursuing their own goals. The Fed is an independent central bank and cannot be forced to monetize the debt.

10. The Fed has direct control over the monetary base because it can change the level of bank reserves immediately through open market operations. The M1 money multiplier depends on the reserve to deposit ratio (*rd*) as well as the ratio of currency to deposits (*cd*). The Fed directly controls the *minimum* value for *rd* through its reserve requirements, but banks may choose to hold reserves above the minimum amount. Individuals control the value of *cd* by choosing how much currency they wish to hold given the amount of their deposits. Thus the Fed can only indirectly control the money multipliers.

12. M1 dropped sharply at the beginning of the Great Depression because of a large decrease in the money multiplier at that time. The multiplier fell because of large increases in the amount of currency held by the public (an increase in *cd*) and in the amount of reserves held by banks (an increase in *rd*). The Fed was actually *increasing* the monetary base at that time, but its efforts were overtaken by the drop in the multiplier. According to Friedman and Schwartz, the Fed should have recognized that the multiplier was dropping and should have taken action to increase the monetary base more dramatically.

14. In 1979, Fed Chairman Paul Volcker changed the Fed's policy target from the federal funds interest rate to the growth rate of the money supply. He announced targets for money supply growth, but the Fed was largely unsuccessful in meeting these targets. Volcker's goal was to allow interest rates to rise as much as necessary to lower inflation. Interest rates did indeed rise dramatically, leading to the worst recession since the Great Depression. At the end of the recession, however, inflation was substantially lower than it had been at the beginning of the Volcker experiment.

16. A *bank run* occurs when widespread fear of a coming bank failure leads depositors to suddenly withdraw cash from the bank. During the Great Depression, bank runs were quite common, and caused many banks to close when their liquid assets were not large enough to cover the depletion of liquid liabilities. The banking panics of the 1930s were largely brought to an end with the institution of deposit insurance. With banks covered by deposit insurance, depositors knew that even if the bank failed, they would not lose their deposits. With the knowledge that they were covered by insurance, depositors no longer had an incentive to panic and withdraw their funds—and the bank runs ceased. In addition to deposit insurance, banks are now more

thoroughly regulated and examined for soundness than they were in the past—largely by the Federal Reserve, the Comptroller of the Currency, and the FDIC.

Numerical Questions

2.   a.   In selling the bond to the Fed, the bank is exchanging one asset (the bond) for another asset (reserves). The money supply consists of bank deposits plus currency held by the public—but in this example we are assuming that individuals do not hold currency. Since there has not been a change in the value of deposits, the Fed's purchase of the bond has not yet affected the money supply.

       b.   What are the values of the first three loans?

The bank initially has $100 in excess reserves, and can loan out the entire amount: the value of the first loan is $100.

With the original loan remaining in the bank, the bank has reserves of $100 and a deposit of $100, leaving excess reserves of $90: the value of the second loan is $90.

The bank now has reserves of $100 and deposits of $190, leaving excess reserves of $81: the value of the third loan is $81.

A total of $271 is created by the first three loans.

       c.   The monetary base increased by $100 when the Fed bought the bond. Since the public holds no currency, there are no further changes in the monetary base.

       d.   What are the values of the first three loans if individuals hold 20 percent of any amount loaned as cash?

The bank initially has $100 in excess reserves, and can loan out the entire amount: the value of the first loan is $100.

After the individual withdraws $20, the bank will have $80 in reserves and $80 in deposits, leaving $72 in excess reserves for the second loan.

After the individual withdraws $14.40, the bank will have reserves of
$65.60 and total deposits of $137.60, leaving excess reserves of $51.84
for the third loan.

A total of $223.84 is created by the first three loans.

Analytical Questions

2. a. Required reserves cannot by themselves guarantee that banks will
        always have sufficient funds to cover withdrawals since they are only a
        fraction of the total deposits. In fact, our banking system is often
        referred to as a "fractional reserve system." Unless the bank maintains
        100 percent reserves, if all deposits are withdrawn, the bank will not
        have sufficient funds to pay its depositors.

    b. Reserve requirements raise the costs of banks because they do not earn a
        return for the bank. When a bank loans out excess reserves, those funds
        generate a return by earning interest. For its required reserves, the bank
        has the choice of holding the reserves as vault cash or as deposits at the
        Fed—neither of which earn interest. Thus, the larger the fraction of
        deposits held as reserves, the smaller the fraction of deposits that can
        earn a return for the bank.

Chapter 15: Saving Behavior and Credit Markets

Review Questions

2.   *Insurance* provides a mechanism for people to avoid *income uncertainty*—it provides a way for the "lucky" to pay off the "unlucky" members of the generation. An insurance program will only be successful if there is no *aggregate income uncertainty* where either *all* members of a generation are lucky or *all* are unlucky. If people buy insurance they will not save as much as they would have saved otherwise, moving the economy to a lower transition curve.

4.   *Bequests* are transfers from one generation to the next that occur at the death of the person making the transfer. Bequests may be *intended* or *unintended*. The larger the level of bequests to each young person in a generation, the higher the transition curve will be for the next period. The transition curve shifts upwards since the young will save at least part of any bequest that they receive.

6.   *Intervivos transfers* are transfers that take place "between the living," most often between parents and children. Some examples given in the text include parents' payment of college tuition, gifts of cars, and low-interest (or no-interest) loans. Intervivos transfers may make the government's intergenerational transfer programs less effective. If the government transfers funds from the child's generation to the parent's generation (or vice versa), the parent may return the transfer to the child as an intervivos gift. A study by Altonji, Hayashi, and Kotlikoff found very little evidence that intervivos gifts affect saving and consumption in the United States.

8.   Individuals are *credit constrained* if they do not have ready access to credit markets and are thus unable to borrow at any interest rate. Credit constraints can arise when the legal system does not provide a way to compel individuals to pay their debts. If borrowers can easily default, then lenders will not issue loans—even at very high interest rates.

10.   *Credit constraints* limit the availability of credit in a given market. Therefore, credit constraints will prevent individuals from borrowing, which tends to raise total saving in the economy. With higher saving, the transition curve will be higher than it would be if more borrowing were allowed.

Numerical Questions

2.   a.   Assume that $A = 10$, $\alpha = 0.4$, and $\beta = 0.3$:

$$\bar{k} = [(1-\alpha)(1-\beta)A]^{\frac{1}{1-\beta}} = [(0.6)(0.7)(10)]^{\frac{1}{0.7}} = 7.7688$$

$$\bar{w} = (1-\beta)A\bar{k}^{\beta} = (0.7)(10)(7.7688)^{0.3} = 12.9481$$

    b.   Assume that each generation gives a bequest of 2 units of output to their offspring. The new transition equation will be:

$$k_{t+1} = (1-\alpha)(1-\beta)Ak_t^{\beta} + 2$$

Period	k	w
0	7.7688	12.9481
1	9.7688	13.8692
2	10.3215	14.1001
3	10.4600	14.1566

Bequests have shifted the transition curve upward by two units, leading to greater saving and a higher capital-labor ratio.

Analytical Questions

2.   a.   The *risk neutral* lender will charge an interest rate that would allow an *average* return of the risk-free 10 percent. To calculate the exact value, we assume that 98 percent of the loans will be repaid, and 2 percent will be defaulted.

$(0.98)(1+r) = 1.10$

$r = 0.1224$ or 12.24%

If the lender is *risk averse*, the interest rate will be even higher since he or she is very worried about potentially bad outcomes (high default rates).

b.   If the lender is *certain* about the default rates of different groups, then interest rates will be set according to those default rates:

black hair: $(0.99)(1+r) = 1.10$

$r = 0.1111$ or 11.11%

red hair: $(0.98)(1+r) = 1.10$

$r = 0.1224$ or 12.24%

blond hair: $(0.97)(1+r) = 1.10$

$r = 0.1340$ or 13.40%

4.   a.   The generational account is equal to the present value of net tax payments. Since the tax is being levied in the current period, the generational account is equal to the amount of the tax, $100.

b.   Since Andy and Ben have borrowed the present value of their future earnings, they must reduce their consumption by $100 each in order to pay the tax.

c.   The generational account for Andy and Ben is unchanged since the present value of the tax is the same ($110/1.10=$100). Since they know that they will have to pay the tax next period, Andy and Ben each will borrow $100 less this period. Thus, their consumption is unchanged as well.

d.   Andy and Ben would prefer to spend more now, but they are unable to because of the credit constraint. In fact, they can only consume $300 in the first period, which leaves $220 for consumption in the second period after they repay their loan. Therefore, they would prefer to pay the tax of $110 in the future. If they pay a tax of $100 now, they can only consume $200 now and $220 in the future. If they pay a tax of $110 in the future, they can consume $300 now and $110 in the future. Since they prefer to consume more in the current period, they would prefer to pay their taxes later.

Chapter 16: Financial Markets and the Investment Decision

Review Questions

2. *Fixed investment* is the purchase of durable goods that are used to produce output. The categories of fixed investment are business fixed investment (which includes producers' durable equipment and non-residential structures) and residential investment (houses, apartment buildings, etc.). *Inventory investment* occurs when a firm acquires goods or raw materials that it will process or is waiting to sell. Examples of inventory investment by an automobile manufacturer would include the following: raw materials used in production (glass, steel, etc.), parts (tires, odometers, etc.), and finished cars waiting to be shipped out.

4. The *user cost of capital* is the total cost to a firm of using a unit of capital for one period (usually a year). The before-tax user cost of capital considers the market interest rate and the depreciation rate. The equation for the basic user cost is simply:

    $$\text{user cost} = r + \delta$$

    The firm decides how much capital to use by setting the marginal product of capital (*MPK*) equal to the user cost:

    $$MPK = r + \delta$$

    That is, firms will choose the amount of capital to use by finding the quantity of capital where the marginal product is equal to the cost of using that additional unit of capital.

6. The *demand schedule for capital* indicates the quantity of capital that a firm would demand at a given real interest rate. It is derived by considering the production function (to get the *MPK*) and the user cost of capital. The demand curve should have a negative slope since an increase in the real interest rate will increase the user cost of capital, which in turn will decrease the quantity of capital demanded. An increase in the rate of depreciation (δ) would shift the demand curve downward since it will increase the user cost of capital at every interest rate. An increase in the tax (τ) per dollar of capital would have a similar effect.

8. Government *investment incentives* are tax subsidies designed to encourage particular types of investment spending. One type of investment incentive is the *investment tax credit* where firms are able to take as a tax rebate a certain fraction of new investment spending. Another investment incentive is *accelerated depreciation allowance*, which allows firms to increase income tax deductions for depreciation. Investment incentives reduce the user cost of capital—generally by reducing the effective tax rate on capital (τ). There are two key reasons why the government might choose to tax corporate income and offer investment incentives at the same time: (1) the corporate income tax is levied on income from *all* sources, but the investment incentives only apply to certain types of corporate investment, and (2) this approach to corporate taxation allows the government to increase taxes on those who currently own capital while lowering the user cost of capital (which attracts new investment).

10. A firm's *financial policy* describes the decisions made by managers regarding how to obtain funds for investment. Firms are limited to borrowing (issuing bonds or borrowing from banks), issuing equity (selling stock), or internally financing investment (using retained earnings). *Securities* are financial assets representing claims on the assets of the firm. *Bonds* are assets that represent debts of the firm. A firms total *debt* is the sum of its loans from banks and the bonds that it has outstanding. *Equity* represents ownership of the firm and is measured as the number of shares of stock outstanding.

12. The *yield spread* is the interest rate gap between bonds issued by large, financially secure companies (companies that have a very high bond rating) and those issued by smaller, or less well known companies. The yield spread indicates that lenders charge a premium for loans to companies that are considered to have higher risk. In times of recession, yield spreads tend to rise.

14. The *irreversibility of investment* refers to the fact that it may be difficult (or even impossible) to reverse an investment decision once it has been initiated. Investments in long-lived capital goods—particularly buildings—are most subject to the problem of irreversibility.

16. *James Tobin's q* represents the costs of adjustment faced by firms making new investment—that is, the full unit costs of acquiring and installing capital. Tobin hypothesized that the rate of investment would depend on the ratio of the market value of capital to its replacement cost. If investment is very high (an "investment boom"), the costs of absorbing all of the new capital should be even higher than usual—so the value of q should rise with the quantity of investment. Fumio Hayashi tested Tobin's theory by comparing the levels of

investment to the value of the firm's stock. The empirical evidence for the theory is mixed, but it appears to have held fairly well in the period following 1990.

Numerical Questions

2. a. For this part of the problem, the user cost of capital is equal to the interest rate. To find the demand for capital, we just set the MPK equal to the real interest rate:

$$r = \beta A k^{\beta-1}$$

and then solve for the value of k.

r	k
0.1	467.84
0.2	147.36
0.3	74.97
0.4	46.42
0.5	32.00
0.6	23.61
0.7	18.26
0.8	14.62
0.9	12.01

  b. With the tax on capital of $\tau = 0.02$, and depreciation of $\delta = 0.10$, we now calculate the user cost as:

$$\text{user cost} = r + \delta + \tau$$

which we set equal to the marginal product of capital:

$$r + \delta + \tau = \beta A k^{\beta-1}$$

and then solve for the value of k.

r	user cost	k
0.1	0.22	125.72
0.2	0.32	67.33
0.3	0.42	42.79
0.4	0.52	29.98
0.5	0.62	22.36
0.6	0.72	17.43
0.7	0.82	14.03
0.8	0.92	11.58
0.9	1.02	9.75

c. The introduction of a tax on capital and capital depreciation raised the user cost of capital at each interest rate and decreased the quantity demanded. Thus, the demand curve was shifted down.

4. a. In this problem we assume that α depends on the real interest rate such that:

$$\alpha = 0.5 - 0.14r$$

We can solve for the supply of capital by substituting the expression above into our normal steady-state capital-labor equation:

$$k = [(1-\alpha)(1-\beta)A]^{\frac{1}{1-\beta}}$$

$$k = [(1-0.5-0.14r)(1-\beta)A]^{\frac{1}{1-\beta}} = [(0.5-0.14r)(1-\beta)A]^{\frac{1}{1-\beta}}$$

Here we will substitute the value of r and then solve for k.

r	α	k
0.1	0.486	6.5342
0.2	0.472	6.8335
0.3	0.458	7.1381
0.4	0.444	7.4481
0.5	0.430	7.7632
0.6	0.416	8.0836
0.7	0.402	8.4092
0.8	0.388	8.7399
0.9	0.374	9.0756

b.   Since α now depends on the real interest rate, we see that a higher real interest rate leads to a larger quantity of capital supplied. In this version of the model, we see that savings are influenced by the interest rate.

Analytical Questions

2.   a.   If the firm raises funds using equity, then the firm's user cost of capital is given by:

$$\text{user cost} = e + \delta + \tau$$

b.   If the firm uses 40 percent debt and 60 percent equity, then the user cost is given by:

$$\text{user cost} = [(0.4)(r) + (0.6)e] + \delta + \tau$$

c.   If the firm can deduct its interest payments, then the part of the user cost attributable to interest on debt should be modified to reflect the new tax deduction:

$$\text{user cost} = [(0.4)(r)(1 - c) + (0.6)e] + \delta + \tau$$